Surviving the baby blues

GW00362520

Surviving
the baby blues

Recognizing, understanding
and overcoming postnatal depression

Jane Feinmann

WARD LOCK

A WARD LOCK BOOK

First published in the UK 1997
by Ward Lock
Wellington House
125 Strand
LONDON
WC2R 0BB

A Cassell Imprint

A British Library Cataloguing in Publication Data block for this book
may be obtained from the British Library

ISBN 0 7063 7624 2
Cover illustration by Lesley Craig
Designed by Paula McCann
Printed and bound in Great Britain by Mackays of Chatham PLC

For Polly and James

Contents

Foreword   9

Introduction   11

1   Postnatal depression – what is it?   15

2   Who is at risk?   43

3   The part professionals play   71

4   Mother and father   84

5   Mother and baby, mother and work   97

6   What support helps?   114

7   Looking after yourself   129

Bibliography   149

Useful addresses   151

Index   155

Foreword

Jane Feinmann has written a much-needed book. Mothers suffering from postnatal depression and also fathers will find it informative as well as comforting. Health visitors and doctors too will find this a comprehensive book on the subject.

Postnatally depressed women often feel desperately lonely, and may find it hard to appreciate help offered. The sympathetic descriptions of emotions and relationships will be recognizable to many; and reading about yourself can be a great help. Understanding postnatal depression goes a long way towards overcoming it.

Dilys Daws,
Child Psychotherapist, The Tavistock Clinic

Introduction

For over 20 years, doctors have mulled over the curiously random nature of postnatal depression. Why should it be that thousands of women every year find the experience of becoming a mother disorientating, disturbing and damaging – instead of finding in parenthood joyfulness, spiritual growth and a new maturity? And why do these women fail to fit the normal pattern of depression? Why does this group include women of all (childbearing) ages and from all social classes and ethnic groups, both women who go out to work and those who look after the home, those who are married and those who are single parents?

Until recently, it was widely believed that it was a woman's hormones that made the difference. During pregnancy, a woman's sex hormones increase by up to 100 times normal levels, then virtually disappear within hours of giving birth. Somehow, it was argued, this dramatic hormonal change affects some women quite differently from normal. Either the hormonal change was greater in some women than in others or the bodies of certain women were, for some reason, less able to process that change. As a theory it was never very plausible (though many hundreds of women appeared to be 'cured' by the administration of progesterone suppositories). Now most doctors accept that if hormones do play a role in postnatal depression, it's a relatively small one.

Over the last five years, there has been a breakthrough in understanding the psychology of childbirth and motherhood. Postnatal depression, it is now widely accepted, has a number of causes. Emotionally, new mothers may all look pretty much the same to the white coats in antenatal clinics and obstetrics wards, but our backgrounds are all different. We have different experiences of being nurtured as babies and children. We have differing abilities to adapt to change – some do it well, some not so well. We have different relationships with our families, our partners, our friends – some of us feel comfortable with the world; others do not. Some of us will experience birth itself as exhilarating and inspiring; others will emerge emotionally scarred. Some will find bonding with their new baby as easy as falling off a log; others experience devastating emotional emptiness.

All these different factors, and more, affect the experience of motherhood, sometimes adversely. And almost all of these factors – obstetric and hormonal apart – affect fathers as well.

No one knows exactly how prevalent postnatal depression is. Official statistics put it at one in ten women but these are 30-year-old 'guesstimates' and there are no up-to-date figures available. Postnatal depression is still something of a taboo subject. It may be that postnatal depression is far more common than has been thought. The Association for Postnatal Illness reported that when Princess Diana broke the silence and talked about 'the bit of a difficult time' she had after the birth of Prince William when she'd 'wake up in the morning feeling you didn't want to get out of bed, you felt misunderstood and just very, very low', thousands of women identified with the description and jammed the switchboard asking for help.

In most, but not all cases, postnatal depression is self-limiting. But that is no reason at all to ignore it. Even relatively short episodes of the condition can be devastating in terms of the mother's ability to bond with her baby and in the relationship between father and mother. One of the great concerns of our times is the breakdown in the family. We hear all the time various pundits decrying the fact that two out of three marriages end in divorce. A factor that is often overlooked is that marital breakdown frequently occurs in the early years of marriage and is often associated with the birth of children, appearing to be triggered by the experience of becoming a parent.

This book contains a number of unhappy stories. But it is

certainly not intended to present a picture of doom and gloom. Perhaps the greatest problem with postnatal depression is its insidious nature, the way that it creeps up on people and takes over their lives so that they are unable to see the difference between the depression and themselves. That process need no longer be inevitable. The new understanding of the causes of postnatal depression has engendered a tremendous sense of optimism among professionals such as health visitors. It is now possible to reach out and identify those couples who are at risk of depression and provide sensitive support to enable them to confront and overcome obstacles in the transition to parenthood.

This book attempts to provide a greater understanding of the condition, its causes and effects as well as information on how to find the support and the therapies to beat it. Becoming a parent involves growth which cannot happen without some pain. But there are many ways in which men and women today can give themselves a head start towards the joyful miracle of parenthood.

CHAPTER 1

Postnatal depression – what is it?

'My friend told me she had postnatal depression. ... I looked at her baby and I got postnatal depression.' This rather tasteless one-liner by Victoria Wood may well be the only existing postnatal depression joke. Even in the upfront 1990s, it's taboo to talk about the disappointment, depression and despair that can follow the birth of a baby.

Most of us don't expect life with baby to be an extended version of a nappy advertisement – with soft focus lights shimmering on an elegantly dressed mother, not a hair out of place, smiling sweetly at her adorable cooing infant. Nor, however, do we expect to experience exhaustion, lethargy, resentment, fear, guilt and panic, not just fleetingly but on a continuous, 'this is what my life's like' basis. Having children, says psychiatrist Ian Brockington, is 'the main purpose of many women's lives – their pride, their passion and their chief reward.' And when that dream goes sour, those around us – friends, relatives and professionals – don't seem to know what to do.

To be told you are suffering from postnatal depression can be a confusing and usually unwanted diagnosis. It's unwanted because it's seen as a stigma, a judgement about being a bad parent rather than a diagnostic tool that can lead the way to recovery. It's confusing for more complicated reasons.

First, there are a number of different explanations for the condition, all of which are at least partly true.

- *The medical model* ascribes the emotional imbalance of some women after childbirth to the hormonal changes occurring at that time.

- *The social model* is based on the view that depression after a birth is a reasonable response to a worsening of social circumstances and unexpected loss of identity as a direct result of giving birth.

- *The psychological model* is based on the identification of risk factors in the woman's personality that are likely to make her vulnerable to depression after the birth of her child.

- *The psychotherapy model* views the experience of becoming a parent as a time of vulnerability to unrecognized trauma from early childhood.

Media coverage of all the different breakthroughs and developments only adds to the confusion. One day we read that a new hormone patch is the answer to postnatal depression; another day we hear that women who suffer from postnatal depression are grieving for a lost body image. One week, we're told that unsupportive partners are a cause of postnatal depression; another week it's supportive partners that make women depressed.

At the same time, newspapers and magazines inevitably focus on the dramatic end of postnatal illness. Headlines such as: 'MUM THREW BABY OUT OF WINDOW', 'BABY BLUES SPARKS BLOODY HAMMER RAGE', 'MOTHER OF FOUR TAKES OVERDOSE', 'MOTHER WHO KILLED HER BABY WALKS FREE' suggest that women risk a dramatic Jekyll and Hyde personality change when they start a family. Even readers of baby magazines can find out how 'BECOMING A MUM TOOK ME TO HELL AND BACK', at the same time as learning how to weave your own Moses basket.

All these headlines actually relate to cases of a relatively rare clinical condition called 'postnatal psychosis', which will be discussed only briefly in this book. Postnatal psychosis is an extreme form of manic depression and can be very dangerous.

Some sufferers become violent or murderous, although in the majority of cases the violence is directed against themselves. The condition follows about one in 500 pregnancies and has existed in about the same numbers since the earliest medical reports. Apart from the fact that both conditions occur postnatally, it has nothing whatsoever to do with the illness known as 'postnatal depression' described in this book.

What is postnatal depression?

The thing about depression, according to former sufferer, Elizabeth Wurtzel, is that it has got nothing to do with life. In her book *Prozac Nation*, she writes:

> *In the course of life, there is pain and sorrow – which in their right time and season, are normal – unpleasant but normal. Depression is an altogether different zone because it involves a complete absence, absence of feeling, absence of response, absence of interest. The pain you feel in the course of a major clinical depression is an attempt on nature's part to fill up the empty space. And the worst thing about it is that if you ask anyone in the throes of a major depression how he got there, he'll never know.*

In her book *Depression: The way out of your prison*, psychologist Dorothy Rowe describes depression as being like a prison in which the sufferer is the cruel jailer as well as the helpless prisoner.

> *When you are unhappy, even if you have suffered the most grievous blow, you are able to seek comfort and let that comfort come through to you to ease the pain. You can seek out and obtain another's sympathy and loving concern; you can be kind and comfort yourself. But in depression, neither the sympathy and concern of others nor the gentle love of oneself is available. Other people may be there, offering all the love, sympathy and concern any person could want, but none of this compassion can pierce the wall that separates you from them, while inside the wall you*

not only refuse yourself the smallest ease and comfort but you also punish yourself by words and deeds.

The distinction between unhappiness and depression is between coping and not coping. You can grieve over the death of a loved one, experience the hurt of being dumped by a boyfriend, cope with the crisis of losing your job or getting into financial difficulties, while at the same time staying in touch with the world around you, drawing comfort from friends and family, keeping a perspective that leaves you intact. But when you become depressed as a result of a setback or a crisis or a negative image you have of yourself, perhaps from something that happened years ago, that event or difficulty in your life hacks away at your self-esteem and undermines your confidence to such an extent that you withdraw into the self-made prison that Dorothy Rowe describes.

Scientists are still unable to explain why and how people become depressed. The most convincing theory is that it happens when the mental balance is upset by one or more 'life events', occurrences that are so emotionally exhausting that they disrupt the chemicals in the brain that maintain mental equilibrium. It's a bit like a points system: if you overload on too many life events, you can – sometimes suddenly, sometimes over a period of months or years – succumb to depression. Examples of these life events include the death of a parent, particularly for a child under the age of 11, the death of a spouse, imprisonment, divorce, unemployment, moving house, changing jobs – and having a baby.

We're led to believe from many quarters these days that childbirth is not a major disruption. Women have babies and within months they're back to editing national papers, campaigning to become the Prime Minister, climbing mountains and running marathons. But just because the physical experience of childbirth has been tamed, it doesn't mean that human beings have become any better at coping with the emotional side of childbirth. In fact, if anything, we seem to have got worse – or at least worse at recognizing these difficult areas, admitting to them, talking about them and confronting them.

Just as most people cope with bereavement, change and

disappointment, emerging battered but unbowed, so almost everyone adjusts to parenthood eventually. Nevertheless, the adjustment period can be long and difficult, with many unhealthy and unwanted steps along the way. The exact number of people suffering from postnatal depression is not known. Experts put it at around one in ten new mothers – but that figure derives from studies carried out 30 years ago which have not been repeated. There is now concern that the current figure is far larger and includes hundreds of thousands of 'ordinary' men and women whose lives, instead of being enriched by the arrival of children, are thrown into turmoil.

The rest of this chapter will look at the kind of adverse experiences that are normally grouped together under the umbrella term 'postnatal depression', although only one section is actually entitled postnatal depression and the first two sections relate to the months before the birth.

Depression which starts during pregnancy

In an ideal world, every pregnant woman would have emotional, domestic and financial security, enjoying excellent health and confident of her ability to meet the challenges of labour and motherhood. Needless to say, we don't live in an ideal world and it rarely works like that. Pregnancy is not always planned, nor always welcomed, often for very good reasons. It can result from inadequate or non-existent contraception, from an unexpected sexual encounter in a short-term relationship or an unhappy, failing relationship. It can threaten a woman's health or her independence or bring to a head long-standing doubts about her partner.

Once established, the pregnancy and its life-changing outcome can cause serious worries about the future – about inadequate housing, about work, income and paying the household bills, about the relationship between the mother-to-be and father-to-be and potential lack of support from family and friends. Signs of physical ill-health, such as raised blood pressure or vaginal bleeding, inevitably cause enormous anxiety, especially if they follow a previous miscarriage or a long history of infertility. Coping with the minor ailments of pregnancy such as morning sickness, heartburn, varicose veins and backache can also be a serious inconvenience, especially for working women.

Most women weather all these problems well. In fact, research shows that women who worry more during their pregnancy frequently adapt to life with a baby more easily than those who sail through without a care in the world. It's as though the worriers have faced the prospects of motherhood realistically and not ducked difficult issues. Nevertheless, it has to be said that this is not always the case.

Sue, 32, was delighted and relieved at first when she became pregnant after 18 months of trying for a baby. 'I was determined everything would be perfect. But it seemed as though there was just one problem after another. We had negative equity on a tiny one-bedroom flat. There seemed no prospect of moving without getting into more debt. Yet there was tremendous pressure to move, quite apart from the size of the flat. Almost the same time as I got pregnant, a noisy family moved into the floor above us, waking us up at night and early in the morning. I knew I'd have to go back to work to pay the mortgage but I was terrified that my new boss would try to get rid of me when he knew I was pregnant. So I was trying to hide the pregnancy at work which was difficult because I was being sick right up to six months. Jeff didn't want to face up to how bad things were and I was having a go at him all the time and most nights we'd end up having rows. My mum didn't help, pointing out all the problems and asking me what I was going to do about selling the flat every time I spoke to her. I began to get so miserable I couldn't bear to think about it all. I'd wake up in the morning and think "What have I done?" At work I felt tired, resentful of people who didn't have my problems and when I got home, the least little thing would make me cry.'

Fiona, 28, had recently been promoted in her job when she found she was pregnant. 'I was so torn. We wanted a baby and I'd gone off the pill and we were using condoms or withdrawal. But it couldn't have happened at a worse time. My promotion meant travelling a lot which was very exciting and suddenly it seemed as though there was a time limit on my freedom to get ahead. I couldn't admit it though, especially to Bill, because if I had, there would have been such dreadful choices to make.'

Jenny, 29, was already depressed when she became pregnant with her second child. 'I didn't realize it at the time. I'd just felt very lonely for a long time, as though my life was a series of hurdles that I had to get over. We hadn't planned the pregnancy but I'd always felt that I had a duty to have another baby because otherwise Julie would be missing out as an only child. The pregnancy made me feel more pessimistic and anxious but I just plodded through it, keeping all my feelings to myself. I'd got stuck in other people's view of me as someone who coped despite all the problems and I felt I had to keep that image up because I couldn't imagine what would happen if I stopped believing I could cope.'

Sue, Fiona and Jenny all came from different backgrounds and had to face different problems. What they had in common was that they found themselves isolated in their inability to talk about their difficult feelings.

Acknowledging changing feelings

Here is a list of feelings that you probably find acceptable and feelings that may make you uncomfortable at different stages in your pregnancy, drawn up by psychiatrist Dr Diana Riley. It's healthy and normal to have the full spectrum of these feelings, but it will always help to identify and talk through feelings that make you feel anxious and worried.

Acceptable feelings	Uncomfortable feelings

First three months

Pleasure at fulfilment of reproductive role	Rejection of or mixed feelings about pregnancy
Pleasure at increased status and attention from family and friends	Perception of fetus as invading and unwelcome
Pleasure at successful transition to adulthood	Fear of fetal abnormality, guilt about drinking or smoking
Increased feeling of well-being	Anxiety about possible repeat miscarriage or guilt about previous termination
Sharing an experience with own mother	Competitiveness with own mother

Second three months

Increased attachment to fetus	Dislike of changing shape
Pleasure at seeing baby on scan	Feeling of loss of attractiveness
Increasing detachment from work commitments	Resentment at limitation of activity and leaving work
Social acceptance by other mothers	Withdrawal of attachment to fetus if the pregnancy is threatened by complications
Beginning preparations for the birth	Loneliness

Last three months

Pleasure as well as realistic anxiety about the impending delivery	Phobic anxiety about labour, hospitals or pain
Coming to terms with loss of status/money	Fear of losing partner
Making stronger links with other mothers	Fear of fetal abnormality or stillbirth
Nesting activities	Anxiety about ability to be a parent

Prenatal depression

In rare cases, an episode of depression unrelated to the pregnancy can cause confusion or even amnesia in the mind of a woman so that she is unable to cope with the stress of childbirth. This is what happened, it is believed, to Caroline Beale, the 32-year-old British woman who hit the headlines in September 1994. On the last day of their holiday in New York, Caroline left her boyfriend and his brothers enjoying a drink in a bar and, complaining of stomach ache, returned to the run-down Manhattan hotel where they were staying. She didn't look pregnant and she hadn't told anyone she was expecting a baby. It is now thought that although she had at one time realized she was pregnant, a severe depression following the death of a close friend had made her 'forget' about it. At 1am she gave birth to an 8lb baby girl in the hotel bath, experiencing fear, panic and pain which can hardly be imagined. Having cut the umbilical cord, she placed the baby in a red plastic bag, cleaned the bath, put the bag in a cupboard and went to bed. Her boyfriend Paul returned later, got into bed and fell asleep beside her.

The next morning, after a final shopping trip, Caroline tied the bag with string, hung it around her neck inside her shirt and accompanied her friends to JFK airport. The baby was discovered by security staff when Caroline was searched after she hesitated at the X-ray machine. She was eventually charged with first-degree murder and held without bail for eight months.

Far from smothering the baby deliberately, as the prosecution alleged, the defence argued that Caroline was so confused and terrified that she didn't even consider whether the baby was alive or dead. It could have been either when she put it in the red bag. As pointed out by the doctors who eventually helped to free her from prison, the fact that she tried to take the tiny body home shows how close she felt to her dead child.

Caroline's depression was not primarily caused by her pregnancy although it coincided with it and led to this tragic sequence of events. Most prenatal depression does not have such devastating consequences, but a woman – especially a young woman or teenager – who is depressed at the time she is pregnant may find it almost impossible to plan for, or take a rational approach to the impending birth.

The baby blues

June was on a high the first few days after she gave birth to her daughter Molly. 'I'd had a lot of worries at the beginning of the pregnancy, but as the months went by, I put them behind me. The birth itself was the climax to a time when the world seemed to revolve around me. I felt euphoric and the baby seemed to add to the glow around me. Then the third or fourth night I had a series of vivid, frightening dreams in each of which something terrible happened to the baby. Once she fell down a bottomless pit. Another time she got caught up in the wheels of a huge express train. Everything that happened was a result of unforgivable carelessness on my part. I woke up after each dream sweating and terrified. The next morning, I felt like a different person, less innocent and carefree. My mood had changed yet I couldn't explain why I felt irritable and anxious. By then my stitches were hurting a lot. I was desperate to be comforted and was devastated when Steve visited two hours later than he'd said. It seemed a betrayal of his promise that we would share the responsibilities. The mood lifted over the next day or so but I was never happy in that same unquestioning way.'

The 'baby blues' affects between 50 and 70 per cent of all newly delivered women, usually between the fourth and tenth day after the birth. It often follows a disturbed night's sleep, sometimes with graphic and alarming dreams. The elation of having given birth, the feeling of closeness to the partner, perhaps the sensation of being a mother and father for the first time, and the feeling of gradually falling in love with the baby are suddenly interrupted by inexplicable negative feelings or what doctors call 'emotional over-activity'. 'It was the inside of me, the emotions wanted to cry, not myself,' said Julie, who spent most of two days crying helplessly towards the end of the first week after delivery.

Often, women feel that they can identify a real cause of unhappiness at this time – perhaps the discomfort, exhaustion, lack of attentiveness from those around. The mother may feel disappointed about the way in which she gave birth or worried about the baby, especially if it is in special care. She may have conflicting feelings about the new human being she has produced. It is thought that less than half of new mothers bond immediately with their new babies and it can be frightening to suddenly become aware of an absence of the anticipated maternal devotion.

Above all, women at this time feel anxious about their ability to cope in the future. It's the end of an intense nine month project and the beginning of an 18 year commitment to someone whose character they know nothing about. Even when there is immediate bonding with the baby, there is still anxiety. BBC presenter Jenni Murray described her feelings after the birth of her son.

It's quite true that you look into this pair of eyes that looks back at you and knows you and you fall in love. But at the end of the day, you're left in a room with this little thing in a plastic box, like a very large goldfish bowl and you lie there and you look at it and you think: God, what have I done? Because whatever you have done in the past, you could change. This is a commitment for life. Even if the child were to die, you could be forever defined as its mother because if he died you would never cease to grieve. It's quite the most terrifying responsibility I've ever faced and it doesn't go away.

Here's a list of feelings that many women go through after the birth of a baby, an almost inevitable part of adjusting to the huge changes taking place. It may help to use this as a checklist over a period of days in the weeks after giving birth, to see whether any of these feelings are becoming more or less overwhelming.

Remember, your health visitor will be happy to talk about any worries or concerns, no matter how trivial they may seem.

	Less than usual	No change	More than usual
Tearful			
Mentally tense			
Unable to concentrate			
Low spirited			
Elated			
Helpless			
Finding it difficult to show feelings			
Lack of alertness			
Forgetful or muddled			
Anxious			
Wishing you were alone			
Brooding on things			
Feeling sorry for yourself			
Over-emotional or changeable in mood			

'Normal craziness' – adjusting to a new baby

New mothers are commonly portrayed as happy, loving, confident and calm. Picturing them as tearful, exhausted, anxious and irritable may not sell disposable nappies but it would be more accurate. It is now recognized that something like the baby blues continues for several months in up to six out of ten new mothers and their partners. In America it's commonly known as 'normal adjustment', though American psychologists Ann Dunnewold and Diane Sanford in their book *Postpartum Survival Guide* point out that a better term might be 'normal craziness'. It is rare, they say, for any woman to breeze through the physical adjustments and hard work of feeding, changing and comforting a baby 24 hours a day, all the while trying to restore her control over her own body.

In Britain, a number of leading women in the field have made the point. Joan Raphael-Leff, a psychoanalyst, believes that there is 'a necessary depression of motherhood', a sane response to the dramatic changes in lifestyle 'in the post-honeymoon days of mothering a tiny baby'. Childbirth expert Sheila Kitzinger makes a similar point. 'Motherhood without emotion,' she says, 'would be a very frightening thing and if you have the positive ones – joy, triumph, ecstasy, it is certain that you will also experience the negative ones – fear, depression and rage.' More recently, Mel Parr, a pioneering researcher, has provided the first evidence that large numbers of men and women who are considered at low risk of depression, nevertheless experience considerable destructive emotional turmoil in the months after having a baby. Her work is discussed further in Chapter 4.

'Normal craziness' is most likely to affect first-time mothers who have to rethink their ideas about who they are – how much of the old, childless self they can retain, what sort of a parent they will be in comparison to the ideal parent they planned to be and how they will measure up to their own mothers. This latter is all the more difficult because a woman today is likely to be embarking on a very different model of motherhood from that of her mother and grandmother.

The first-time father faces similar dilemmas. He may be taking on extra responsibility for earning money, with a 'New Man' workload that cuts into the time he previously had for himself and his own activities – all for the child of a woman who may suddenly no longer look or act like the woman he fell in love with and who may have little time or affection to spare. 'Having a baby is like taking in a lodger and finding your wife is sleeping with him,' one father remarked.

Although it is apparent to most couples that their relationship will change after the birth of a baby, it is not that easy to plan for. 'It is hard to make plans in advance when the baby's personality and the mother's condition after childbirth are a big unknown,' say Ann Dunnewold and Diane Sanford. 'All the ground rules for a household and a relationship change when a baby arrives. It's rare for a couple to simply know the right adjustments to make to find their sense of balance again.'

Unhappily, traditional antenatal classes rarely touch on this common emotional response to early parenthood, concentrating on practical skills such bathing the baby, changing the nappy, breastfeeding and above all, preparing for the birth itself, regarded as the be all and end all of antenatal education – instead of the beginning of new, uncharted territory.

According to Dunnewold and Sanford, all the following feelings and experiences are acknowledged to be part of 'normal adjustment' for a parent in the first few months of a baby's life:

- Crying and tearfulness

- Irritability

- Anger

- Sleep disturbance

- Fatigue

- Negative mood

- Appetite changes

- Loss of interest in usual activities

- Loss of interest in sex

- Anxiety

- Mood swings

- Feelings of doubt about attractiveness and parenting skills.

Writing in *Vogue*, Fiona Golfar recalled the day that 'the post-natal bliss bubble burst' and she saw her reflection in the mirror:

> *or rather not me but a woman wearing a nightdress I wouldn't be seen dead in, with pique edging and buttons down the front. To add to the horror her breasts were hanging out of the feeding bra she was wearing and they seemed mortifyingly to have become the size of two footballs. All I could think about were my nipples and the pain they were in. The worst of it was that what had been an enormous and rather wonderful bump, when dressed and shown off under stretchy fashion numbers, had become nothing more than a huge mass of wobble that looked as if a tiger had clawed it. Welcome to motherhood.*

She describes the moment of despair when she realized that she was no longer attractive to her boyfriend.

> *One morning as I was hauling myself into a pair of knickers made out of J cloth material which would have fitted an elephant, I noticed that my boyfriend was staring at me with a look, not even of disbelief but of total blankness. I had become a 'thing' and nothing could persuade me otherwise.*

She felt cut off from childless friends. Having set up a dinner date with a group of girlfriends, the occasion failed to live up to its promise:

> *Two hours and four calls to the baby-sitter later, after talking about things that simply failed to interest me – who cares about Melinda's coke problem in New York for God's sake and why didn't anybody have anything to say about sore nipples – I confessed that I was miserable and guilty for feeling that way.*

And yet having rushed home, she found that motherhood was equally alien. 'My baby was an eating, sleeping mystery to me.'

There is a connection between 'normal adjustment' and post-natal depression. People who ignore or repress these difficult feelings will find it more difficult to adapt to changes. It may well be that women who succumb to postnatal depression tend to be those who find this period of adjustment particularly difficult. Perhaps they are more isolated and therefore less able to confide in other people, or perhaps they have to cope with more problems. Maybe, for one reason or another, they are frightened or over-judgemental of their own 'crazy' emotions,

Postnatal depression

Postnatal depression is not usually a sudden event. You don't wake up one morning and find you've got postnatal depression. It's a slow, insidious process. You sometimes feel well and happy, then miserable and gradually you have more miserable days than happy days. A woman may make an appointment to see her GP or health visitor because she is feeling so wretched – and then when the day comes she may feel better and assume it was a passing mood, only to find herself engulfed in depression for days.

It's easy to imagine the depressed parent sitting quietly weeping in a corner. But depressed people don't always act like victims, even if that's what they are. Sadness and grief play a heart-rending part in postnatal depression. So does anger, which may be directed at the partner, older children or the baby, and so does an inability to cope with day-to-day chores such as cleaning the house or looking after the children. It's perhaps not surprising that medical staff, friends and family often mistake postnatal depression for mothers behaving badly. Some common symptoms are illustrated in the following examples.

CRYING AND TEARFULNESS
You are sad a lot of the time. It may not affect you every day or for all of every day. You may wake up feeling fine and find that your mood deteriorates as the day drags on. You may feel tearful and cry a lot of the time, sometimes provoked by a story about an accident or disaster on the news. 'I listened to a radio programme about young people today, about how they have no

prospects and end up as criminals. It seemed unutterably depressing. I looked down at my daughter and thought how could I have brought her into this dreadful world?' recalls Joan.

GUILT AND INADEQUACY
You feel guilty and inadequate that you are the only mother in the world who cannot cope.

Marian constantly compared herself to other 'ideal' mothers whose babies would sleep contentedly while they tidied the house and made dinner for their husbands. 'My husband would come home and find me tearful and dishevelled with the baby screaming, nothing in the house to eat and the place a tip. The guilt was almost unbearable.' She felt totally inadequate as a mother, 'me who'd been a competent teacher now couldn't even cope with one baby!'

LOSS OF INTEREST IN USUAL ACTIVITIES
Socializing becomes increasingly difficult and normal social events become an ordeal.

When Michelle became depressed after her second baby, friends rallied round and told her to give them a ring or call round whenever she felt down. 'They might as well have asked me to fly to the moon,' she says. 'I was completely absorbed in my misery. I couldn't face seeing other people and the physical act of talking was sometimes overwhelmingly difficult.'

LACK OF BONDING
Bonding with your baby may simply seem not to happen – again causing feelings of guilt and shame.

Rachel felt 'utterly ashamed' about her lack of feelings for her newborn baby. 'I'd have endless visitors coming to coo over little Nicholas. I could remember making the same kind of visits myself when people had babies and assuming, without even thinking about it, that the mother was dotty about the baby. But at the time, I just wished I could get him adopted or that someone would take him away and not bring him back.'

ANGER

Like the mother described in the following example, you may find that you actively resent your baby.

Susanna remembers the feeling of pleasure when she started haemorrhaging and had to go back into hospital two weeks after her daughter was born. 'I loved it simply because Jessamy wasn't there,' she told the *Telegraph Magazine*. Back at home, she was incapable of looking after the baby. One day, trying to change the baby's nappy as she squirmed and screamed, Susanna picked her up and said 'I hate this baby!' What was so upsetting, she says, was the belief that her life had changed for ever to this exhausting routine of nappy changing and night feeding. 'I couldn't remind myself that Jessamy would grow up and change. And I thought I'd spoilt everything Brett and I had ever had. I don't think I'd have hurt Jessamy but the despair and guilt were unbelievable.'

ANXIETY

New mothers often feel panicky over whether the baby is putting on enough weight or whether a raised temperature is just a cold or possibly meningitis. Depressed mothers can find such fears overwhelming, experiencing classic panic attacks with feelings of dread, palpitations, difficulty in breathing and trembling. They can happen for different reasons but there is a basic lack of confidence in the mother's ability to sustain the child.

Christine, 24, worked in a nursery and adored her baby from the moment it arrived. But she found motherhood quite different from what she expected. She began to have panic attacks when she found her daughter had lost 2lb of her birth-weight at three weeks. 'I was frightened of feeding her and felt panicky when she cried. I was checking her nappy every ten minutes or so. I was staying awake all night to watch her. I was so frightened I couldn't eat.'

Mary, 31, was anxious throughout her fourth pregnancy. She'd had a miscarriage the year before, for which she felt in some way responsible. 'From the moment she was born, I was terrified she was going to die. My stomach churned whenever I heard her cough and I'd lie awake listening to her breathing at night. I actually didn't sleep for nights on end.'

Sharon, 34, felt depressed after her baby was born prema-turely. When her husband was unexpectedly made redundant two months after the birth, she became extremely anxious. On a weekend trip to get away from it all, the couple left the baby with his mother. But that evening, Sharon began to have trouble catching her breath and thought she was going to die. She kept on having severe chest pains and breathlessness until a doctor realized she was having panic attacks and she was able to get effective treatment.

IRRITABILITY

'I'd always had a rather stormy relationship with Bill,' recalls Kate. 'But it got seriously out of hand once the baby arrived. I was anxious about everything – what sort of a mother I'd be, whether I'd be able to go back to work, how our lives were going to turn out. My everyday emotion was a sort of persistent hysteria and I took it all out on Bill. I'd end up hitting him or lashing out with vicious insults. I couldn't bear him coping with things and feeling relaxed while I was so worried. And after being the strong one for so many years, I couldn't stand the idea that I might be dependent on him.'

EXHAUSTION

Jennifer, trying to explain how difficult it was to wash and feed the baby even though she knew it had to be done and wanted to do it very much, described feeling 'as if my feet were stuck in treacle'. The conviction that every other new mother is coping happily and well is almost always part of the illness. Psychologist Dorothy Rowe says that for many depressed women there seems to be a book of rules of housekeeping which was handed down to Moses at the same time as the Ten Commandments. 'While it is possible to break all the Ten Commandments and still be forgiven by God, infringements of the Heavenly Housekeeping Book with its one Universal Law – Your home must be perfectly clean and tidy at all times – is unforgivable.' She understands, she says, 'the terrible despair you can feel when keeping the house clean is just beyond your strength or when your life is going badly awry, you obsessively clean and tidy your house since this is the only part of your life that you can control and keep in order.'

This view is one that we, as representatives of society, tend to endorse. If we visit a friend who has recently had a baby, we feel full of admiration when we find the house tidy and the baby cooing contentedly, and 'tut-tut' to ourselves when the house is a mess and the baby crying. 'We all do it, I'm afraid,' admitted one leading health visitor, 'even health visitors who know about postnatal depression and who should know how destructive such attitudes are.'

Rowe's advice is to recognize that keeping the house clean is part of a defence against your own view of yourself as bad. 'Over the years I became able to live with a degree of untidiness and dirt,' she says. Such a philosophy is something that well-adjusted mothers should adopt without a second's thought.

INABILITY TO COPE

You may have an overwhelming sense that you are not coping with day-to-day activities, something that hits you particularly hard if you've led an active, energetic and capable working life.

'I had to go back to work when my son was three months,' says Joyce. 'I made a total mess of the childcare arrangements. I toiled round childminders and interviewed day nannies, but the whole time I felt as though I wasn't in control. I felt pessimistic as though I was going to make bad choices – which I did. I couldn't decide what to wear, when to feed the baby, when to do the housework. I felt devoid of confidence and very tense.'

SLEEP DISTURBANCE

You may find it difficult to get off to sleep at the end of the day and, when woken by the baby, find it hard to get back to sleep. Or you may go into a state of hibernation, wanting to sleep all day and never waking refreshed.

LOSS OF INTEREST IN FOOD

You may go off your food or simply find it impossible to find time to sit down and eat a meal. 'I remember my sister-in-law holding the baby once while I ate my dinner. It felt like such a luxury I could have flung my arms around her and wept,' recalls Pamela. Or you may nibble all day on whatever comes to hand, putting on weight and never having the kind of pleasurable appetite that's part of an ordered routine.

LACK OF CONCENTRATION

The ability to concentrate can disappear – you forget why you went to the shops or what you went upstairs for. It's difficult to read or keep up with ordinary conversations; even keeping up with the TV is a struggle. Judy said that two years after the birth of her baby, she still felt 'a bit vague and sometimes had lapses of memory'. Anne says that in retrospect, she realizes she experienced a great deal of mental confusion. 'The greatest concentration and willpower were required for even the simplest jobs.'

LOSS OF INTEREST IN SEX

The normal loss of interest in sex after the birth of a baby is likely to be more intense and long-lasting. 'Having a kiss and a cuddle were an important part of our lives before the baby, not just as an expression of love but a way of making up when we'd quarrelled,' says Karen. 'But afterward, sex seemed like one more task that would keep me from sleeping. I'd flinch if Alan so much as put his arm round me.'

Grey woman syndrome

↭ ↭ ↭

Vicky, 40, became depressed after the birth of her third child nine years ago. No one realized she was ill and she remained untreated for six years. During that time, she lost her job, her marriage broke up and her three children were put into care. Eventually the Social Services contacted her GP who tried to provide treatment and eventually referred her to hospital. She seemed a hopeless case. Yet the psychiatrist who finally cured her of the depression, after treating her intensively as a hospital in-patient for six months, says that if Vicky's depression had been picked up soon after it started and she had received effective therapy, she would still have a job and a family today.

The consequences of Vicky's depression were unusually severe. In most cases, women with postnatal depression recover within a few months. Eight out of ten get better within a year or eighteen months and, although during that time their life may well have fallen apart, sometimes irreparably, they do get the chance to rebuild from a fresh start when they're better. However, for the unlucky few there's no short-term recovery. Between 10 and 20 per cent of sufferers get stuck in the depression, so that even twenty years later, they have become used to a life that's been grey for as long as they can remember. Once depressed, it is far easier for women to slip into a depressed lifestyle. 'If our eating and sleeping habits are very poor, we soon begin to feel permanently tired and run down,' says psychologist Gerrilyn Smith. 'We forget what it's like to be on top of things and worst of all, we start thinking that it's normal for us to feel like this all of the time.'

Barbara became depressed after the birth of her second child, feeling helpless, dull and panicky and crying often. 'I was frightened for years and yet passive and weary. It was the opposite of the "Seize the day" attitude to life. I could feel the fear in my stomach when I woke up and sometimes it would be there all day. There were reasons for it – rows with my husband, bills that we couldn't pay, problems with the children at school, real problems that I got used to being overwhelming. Everything was an effort and I lost all self-confidence. I had nothing to lose by seeking help but it never occurred to me to talk about the way I was feeling. In fact if ever I was asked, I'd grab the opportunity to convince the questioner as well as myself that I was doing well. It wasn't until many years later, after I was divorced and going through a particularly rocky period that I did go for help and was put on a short course of antidepressants. Within a few weeks, I began to recall what it was like to enjoy life, feel easy with myself, sleep at night instead of worrying and not look at the world through resentful eyes. Instead of leaving bills and bank letters unopened, I was able to get my finances in order and I realized I could take control of relationships with children, family, friends and colleagues at work. It was a revelation.'

No matter how old your children are, if you recognize yourself in the following list, you may be suffering from long-term post-natal depression and will respond to therapy:

- You feel low, generally fed up and weary.

- You have no interest or pleasure in normally enjoyable things.

- You suffer from at least four of the following:
    * disturbed sleep
    * loss of appetite
    * reduced concentration
    * fatigue
    * feeling worthless
    * morbid thoughts.

Postnatal psychosis

Jackie did everything she could think of to prepare for her first pregnancy, including attending yoga and National Childbirth Trust classes in the area. The birth went well and Jackie and her husband congratulated themselves on a perfect start to parenting. 'The problems began when I started to breastfeed. I remember getting terribly anxious, waking at 5am and worrying. Then I started talking intensely all the time. I began to feel that I could manage perfectly without sleep provided I kept up with my yoga. I felt as though I was finding out the secret of the universe. I talked non-stop about my discoveries and wrote poetry and loads and loads of notes about reaching 'the final frontier'. I've still got some of them and they don't make much sense. Fortunately I realized there was something wrong with me and agreed to see a doctor and was successfully treated. But when I had my second child two years later, exactly the same thing happened.'

Postnatal or puerperal psychosis is an extraordinary condition – the most severe of all forms of insanity, many psychiatrists believe. It is also relatively rare, occurring in only one in every 500 births. There is a dramatic contrast between the rationality and calm of the woman through the ordeal of childbirth, and the disorientation, delusions, hallucinations and perplexity experienced as the psychosis takes hold, usually within the first two weeks after the birth.

Anne Broadbent told the *Observer* that friends told her she was manic after the birth of her fourth child at the age of 34.

'I thought I was just happy. I remember I gave a dinner party the night before he was born and another one the night after.' She'd stay up all night, 'sewing, reading and cooking – just doing the things that I do normally but I couldn't stop doing them. I never stripped in public or went on wild spending sprees like some do. But I talked all night, made endless connections between apparently disconnected things. I punned all the time – that's very common. I thought I was just being me but more so and more wonderfully so.' These episodes of mania would be interspersed with long periods of depression. She would lie for weeks, months on end in bed, a prisoner in her house, not able to do anything. 'People

*tell you to pull yourself together but I didn't have anything to pull
with. And I felt bitterly ashamed. I wanted to die.'*

Although cases of this illness have been reported by doctors
since the dawn of medicine, it is still not fully understood. Until
recently, it was believed to be a form of schizophrenia. Now most
view it as a form of manic depression with spells of hyperactive
euphoria being followed by episodes of 'depthless despair'.
Although it is widely thought to be triggered by the fall in
hormones after the birth in certain vulnerable women, there have
been reports of psychosis in women following adoption of a
baby. Some psychiatrists believe that it is a severe form of the
baby blues and there are incidences of postnatal psychosis being
mistaken for the less severe condition.

Some women become over-active and restless – a whirlwind
of energy yet easily distracted. They make lists of things to do,
then jump up to clean the house or start packing to go on a holiday, and then suddenly become irritable, suspicious or depressed, all in a matter of hours. When her husband came home one
evening, Nancy was outside the house washing the car while
inside there was wet laundry on the sofa and rice burning in a
pan on the stove.

Other women become lethargic, unable to cope with the
physical demands of motherhood, and tend to withdraw into
a delusional state.

∾ ∾ ∾

Vivienne was diagnosed as suffering a mild version of postnatal
psychosis when her second child was 18 months. 'I'd become
obsessed with the belief that two or three of my neighbours
were abusing their children. So much so that I actually reported
them to social services. I'd stand at the window for hours
watching for signs of the evil that I felt was all around me.'

Lucy remembers her baby's eyes changing colour when she
looked at him, convincing her that he was the child of the

devil. She kept feeling his forehead to check that he wasn't growing horns.

Pauline became convinced that she understood the secret of life. 'I felt as though I had the power to save the world and I tried to contact politicians to tell them how to prevent war and famine.'

Symptoms of psychosis

Postnatal psychosis is the most dangerous of all postnatal conditions. It can end in the suicide of the mother or even the murder of the baby. Anyone with any of the symptoms listed below should always seek immediate help from their GP.

- Feeling speeded up

- Little need for sleep or rest

- Distractibility

- Speech seems very fast, pressured, tripping over words

- Irritability

- Easily excited

- Delusions and visions.

Conclusion

Postnatal depression is not a scientifically exact term, neither is it an illness, as we normally understand the word. Doctors use the term to describe a number of different symptoms occurring with varying severity. But these symptoms are most usefully perceived as normal feelings, normal responses to a changing, sometimes uncontrollable situation. As we shall see later in the book, these feelings and reactions are more likely to develop into clinical depression when they are internalized and repressed. Understanding the way that you are feeling and acknowledging it to other people or another person, even if there's nothing that can be done about it, is the only adequate response. As Mel Parr, a pioneer in the field, puts it, in this situation 'Silence is NOT Golden'.

CHAPTER 2

Who is at risk?

Katharina Dalton, a London gynaecologist and one of the first doctors to research and treat postnatal depression, came to the conclusion in her book *Depression After Childbirth*, first published in 1980, that it strikes indiscriminately. Long before Princess Diana revealed to the world in her famous BBC TV *Panorama* interview that she had suffered severe bouts of postnatal depression, Dr Dalton pointed out that the illness:

> *attacks royalty, nobility and famous media personalities as well as the typist, the factory worker and the shop assistant; it can affect the happily married woman, the single mother, the flat dweller, the squatter and those caught in the poverty trap. It strikes at those who have a much-wanted child including women who have endured years of attendance at infertility clinics and at those for whom pregnancy was an unwelcome interruption in their well-ordered lives. It affects equally regular attenders at antenatal clinics and mothers who have spurned all medical help during their pregnancies. It comes unexpectedly into families who have a clean bill of health and have never before had to cope with a psychiatric illness. It can touch the few who have a still-born baby but also the many who have a healthy child.*

The observation led Dr Dalton to conclude that postnatal depression is 'an exclusive disease limited to mothers . . . which occurs towards the end of the reproductive cycle because of an upset of the hormonal balance.' The imbalance happens, she said, when the hormone progesterone, 'nature's natural anti-depressant', which in pregnancy increases to between 50 and 100 times the level of a normal menstruating woman, drops suddenly to insignificant levels within hours of the delivery of the baby. Dr Dalton concluded that women who develop postnatal depression have higher than average progesterone levels during the last few weeks of pregnancy and lower than average after the birth.

During the 1970s and 1980s, Dr Dalton probably did more than anyone else to bring postnatal depression to the public's attention. She described the condition in detail and explained for the first time how pervasive and extensive it is. Her success in treating women with a history of postnatal depression by giving them progesterone suppositories or injections from the day after birth was well publicized. It led to a widespread and persistent view that postnatal depression is a dramatic form of pre-menstrual syndrome (PMS) – that it's purely a question of hormones.

The medical profession, though still actively investigating the potential for hormone therapy, has remained sceptical about the Dalton theory. Attempts by other doctors to repeat her success have failed – progesterone has been shown to be no more effective than placebo. Although women's hormones undoubtedly plummet in the hours after giving birth, there is no evidence that women who become depressed experience a more dramatic reduction than women who do not. What's more, it's now clear that it's not just newly delivered mothers that suffer postnatal depression – men develop symptoms too and so do women who adopt.

There is a suspicion that the caring, maternal character of the pioneering Dr Dalton, combined with her enthusiasm for her philosophy of care, may have had an effect on her results. In any case, in later years she herself admitted that her theory of post-natal depression did not entirely explain the phenomenon. Real postnatal depression, she claimed, affects new mothers 'regardless of social standing or financial security'. There are others, she admitted, 'whose security financial or otherwise has less solidity . . . such as single mothers or those with poor housing conditions or unstable relationships' who might get depressed postnatally, though not with her version of postnatal depression.

Such distinctions are now recognized as unhelpful. Research today tends to support Dr Dalton's original thesis that postnatal depression does indeed strike at random: that some women sail through pregnancy and childbirth even though circumstances seem against them, while others, who might seem to have every-thing going for them, succumb. It seems to be impossible to determine from a woman's age, class, marital status or number of children whether or not she is vulnerable.

Nevertheless, the view today is that hormones are at best only a small part of the story. New research based on the study of women who have suffered clinical depression has led to the iden-tification of a list of risk factors which may help to post up a warn-ing about what kind of emotional responses to expect. These risk factors can be divided into four main categories: social, biological, psychological and those that have to do with relationships.

Social factors

New pressures on parents

It's not known whether postnatal depression was as common prior to the 1960s, when it was first identified and studied, as it is today. It may be that emotional illness was masked by the far higher risk of death during labour for both women and their babies before the Second World War. In those days survival itself was a triumph and emotions took second place. But it may also be no coincidence that postnatal depression has come to promi-nence during a time of change in family life in Western countries. Consider the following well-documented sociological shifts:

- Childbearing and marriage are becoming separate, with more couples having babies outside marriage and a rise in the number of single parents.

- Women are having their first baby at an older age and there are more births to couples who have older children from a previous relationship.

- The number of women returning to work after childbirth is increasing while the number of men in full-time work is decreasing.

At the same time, many Western women have come to believe not only that they *can* have it all – jobs, children, fun, passion – but that they *should* have it all. There are plenty of role models for successful have-it-all women: Pamela Anderson and Madonna are just the latest celebrity mums to pose, slender, sexy and poised with their tiny offspring before effortlessly picking up the threads of their glamorous existences. 'Madonna has shown us all that you can be a mother and a successful woman. If she can do it, we can do it,' was how one tabloid journalist greeted the superstar's new maternal role.

Women today work later into pregnancy and plan to start work earlier than ever before. It's often for financial reasons (surveys show that money is the biggest worry for new mums) or because of pressure from employers. But it may also reflect the new conviction that women can and should take everything in their stride. And there are other changes which result in less support for new mothers. They spend less time in hospital than before, perhaps a day compared to a week a few years ago and several weeks' confinement a generation or so ago. Many would choose not to stay in hospital, which they see as an unfriendly environment, but they are certainly not encouraged to do so by the new management-orientated NHS. And they are less likely to have their mother or other female relatives around to give them tender loving care in the weeks after the birth – many grannies and aunts are at work themselves or live too far away to visit regularly in homes that are anyway too small for them to stay in easily.

The reality is not a brave new world of independent, power-dressed women carrying their babies high as they stride out of the maternity wards to settle the infant in an airy nursery before returning enriched and fulfilled to give their all to the workplace. The reality is all too often a sudden transition to a life of isolation, exhaustion, disappointment and anxiety.

'Society seems to expect new mothers to adapt to an isolated existence within their own homes and to give up their previous freedom without regret or sadness', says Dr Diana Riley, a pioneer in identifying the risk factors for postnatal depression. She believes that by going along with the view that childbirth is a relatively minor interruption to normal life rather than a cataclysmic change, women have lost many benefits, vital support as well as peace of mind and a feeling of well-being in the months immediately after the birth. Statistics show that in traditional societies postnatal depression is less common and, when it does occur, less severe. This is so even in modern, highly developed yet still traditional societies like Japan, where childbirth is taken seriously, antenatal preparations are laborious and women almost always return to their own mother's home after childbirth, often for the first few months.

Financial or housing worries

Social and financial problems are almost always made worse by the arrival of a new baby, who inevitably brings new financial demands at the same time as restricting the mother's freedom to work. When people are placed for a long time in a situation they feel they can neither influence nor escape from, the chances of their becoming depressed are much greater. A woman who is powerless to improve income or housing when it's clearly needed for a new baby, develops, over a period of time, 'learned helplessness'. Such an attitude can be helpful if it enables the woman to relax and accept that she can only do what is possible. But it can lead to depression if it becomes a source of guilt, shame and resentment.

⊲⊳ ⊲⊳ ⊲⊳

Sally was 23 when she became pregnant with her third child. 'My eldest, a son, was five and had behavioural and learning difficulties. My daughter was only one. And we were living in a one-bedroomed flat, just about coping. I was desperate

47

when I found out I was pregnant again. It was the last thing I wanted. I did think for a long time about having an abortion but I decided it would mess me up more than having another baby. When I knew it was too late to go back on my decision, I felt trapped. The whole situation seemed impossible. We couldn't get a larger flat. I felt so resentful towards that baby even after it arrived. And though we did finally move when the baby was still tiny, it didn't improve the situation. We had more room but we'd moved a long way from friends and my mother. Sometimes I hated the baby so much that I couldn't even bear to feed it. My husband used to give it a bottle when he got home from work. It was such a mess.'

Cultural or religious pressures

A woman who finds it easy and acceptable to base her approach to mothering on the way she was mothered, and who feels happy that she is fulfilling the expectations of her own family, will inevitably feel more relaxed and confident about her own ability to be a mother. However, a sudden break with tradition, or conflict between children and their parents or in-laws over whether traditional values should be paramount, makes becoming a mother that much more difficult.

Statistics suggest that women from Asian and other traditional communities who live in the West suffer less from postnatal depression than the indigenous population. It may be that life within a traditional culture remains protective even in another country. However, there is some concern that women from families who have come from countries as diverse as Ireland and India experience higher rates of postnatal depression than is shown by the statistics. It may be that some communities lack the vocabulary or the experience to describe feelings of depression – or the condition may simply not be regarded as legitimate by older members of the family.

Health care personnel may well be less responsive to the

feelings of women from other cultures. Midwives in one large British hospital, for instance, believed that the Asian women in their care 'tended to make a fuss about nothing' and lacked maternal instinct. Yet according to Esther Craddock, an expert in postnatal depression, Asians are used to sharing their concerns with a trusted health carer but at the same time don't find it easy to show affection in front of others or to discuss their feelings.

Obstetric problems

Difficult births

There is no clear evidence that women who have births involving medical interventions are more prone to postnatal depression. Over half of all births involve some intervention: a Caesarean, whether emergency or planned, a forceps delivery or an episiotomy which requires stitches – all of which can sometimes lead to a feeling of failure on the part of the mother and a feeling of loss of control on the part of the father. This reaction is usually short-lived, passing into oblivion within days of the delivery. But there are exceptions. Having an emergency Caesarean can cause a sense of violation, loss of control and failure that can lead to long-term depression, according to research psychologist, Sarah Clement. What is crucial, she believes, is the quality of support and understanding available to the woman and, in the rush of an emergency, that may not be a priority. A woman may feel sad about not taking an active part in the birth of her child: 'as though I spent a long time baking a very special cake, then through no fault of anyone, someone else had to come along, take it out of the oven and ice it.' She may feel inadequate that she's 'failed as a woman,' or was 'bodily deformed so that I couldn't produce my child like a real mother would'.

One woman quoted by Dr Clement recalled an argument with her mother-in-law over how much milk the baby needed. 'I said: "Don't mind me, I'm only his mother," and my mother-in-law said, "But you're not his mother. You never gave birth to him. You took the easy way out, you just lay there and did nothing." I tried to explain that I'd wanted to give birth naturally but it was too dangerous and why did it matter how he'd arrived, that I loved him, but the words wouldn't come out. Deep down I agreed with her.' A woman is at risk of depression, says Dr Clement, if these sad and angry feelings remain unexpressed and are turned inwards onto the self.

Pain and discomfort are recognized by most women as part and parcel of giving birth and any distress after the birth is not usually long-lasting. However, a sizeable minority of women, possibly one in a hundred or more, suffer post-traumatic stress after childbirth. The experience is similar to that first described by Vietnam War veterans, with flashbacks, difficulties in sleeping and nightmares, irritability, panic attacks or depression. Some women are so distressed that they cannot contemplate ever having a smear test, sex, a future vaginal delivery, or even another pregnancy. It has been known for a woman to have a much wanted pregnancy aborted in order to avoid the trauma of another delivery.

Research once again shows that it is not the events themselves that cause the distress but the way that the delivery is handled by unsympathetic medical staff. The women feel violated not by the birth but by a feeling of being ignored or powerless or being victims of hostility from the clinical staff.

Previous infertility

Prolonged infertility can, understandably, be a major cause of depression. As well as longing for a baby which you cannot conceive, there is the feeling of shame and inadequacy felt by both partners that they are incapable of fulfilling their gender roles. Treatment for infertility inevitably causes tremendous emotional turmoil, particularly when it involves therapies that include hormonal treatment, leading to the emotional mood swings that accompany hormonal changes. Couples describe living through a rollercoaster ride of hope followed by bitter disappointment, repeated with each cycle. Yet once a new baby arrives, it's easy to assume that the depression will melt away to be replaced by unbounded joy. Indeed such assumptions are often made by infertility support groups and by fertility experts.

But research shows that women who have a baby after repeated unsuccessful attempts to become pregnant may be at risk of depression when the baby arrives. There are several reasons for this. The simplest is that many women find there is a big gap between the feeling of fulfilment they had hoped for and the reality of the new baby. The dream and the reality simply don't match up. Also, having invested so much of your time, emotional energy and, perhaps, money into having a baby, it's easy to believe that becoming a mother will solve all your problems and leave you living happily ever after. But having your dream fulfilled won't turn you into someone else. You'll still be the same person, with the same fears, regrets, insecurities and limitations. All the problems that were pushed to the background and seemed unimportant compared to the overwhelming distress of infertility will now re-emerge. You'll have the same partner and be prone to the same arguments. The difference will be that you'll have a baby and all the normal stresses of a first-time parent.

Parents who have experienced infertility sometimes find that the normal stresses and strains of parenthood seem unbearable. Not only did they have difficulties getting pregnant, now they have negative feelings about the baby. American psychologists Ann Dunnewold and Diane Sanford found that this was a common experience.

It's easy to come to the mistaken conclusion that there's something the matter with you as a woman for being anything less than ecstatically happy all the time. . . . 'If I were in working order as a woman, I would have been able to get pregnant sooner,' you may tell yourself; or 'I would love every moment of being a mother if I weren't so deficient'. The reality of motherhood as a difficult, demanding, exhausting job can get lost in the crossfire of self-doubt and blame.

Adoption

Parents who adopt a baby or child can experience similar emotional conflict. They too have normally faced long periods of infertility. Furthermore their experience of childlessness may end abruptly with a call from an adoption agency to pick up the baby tomorrow or soon after.

'It just wasn't enough time,' said Dorothy, mother of three adopted children. 'Each time, we were given at most a week to adjust to the idea. Of course we were overjoyed. But there was a terrible tension, a feeling that we hadn't prepared emotionally for the arrival of a baby – so much less than the normal nine months! And apart from anything else there was a terrible rush getting all the baby gear which we couldn't possibly have started until we knew the baby was on its way.'

Like many adoptive parents, Dorothy also assumed that as she'd not actually gone through the process of labour and childbirth, she wouldn't need to take any special care of herself in the early months of motherhood. 'I expected to go on as usual and I didn't make allowances for the exhaustion of getting used to a new baby,' she says. 'I certainly didn't dream of asking for help and the effort of keeping the house clean and entertaining all our guests as well as the sleepless nights eventually got too much for me.'

Biological factors

A woman's body undergoes tremendous hormonal changes from the moment she becomes pregnant. By the time she is three months pregnant, the placenta in her womb is producing up to 50 times the amount of oestrogen and progesterone that is usually in the body. They make possible the huge physical changes which sustain the mother and baby, and produce the 'glow' or feeling of well-being that many women experience in the middle of pregnancy. After the birth, the levels of hormones fall dramatically to about 1/100th of the levels present during pregnancy. At the same time, the body starts to produce high levels of prolactin, the hormone involved in breastfeeding – and they remain high for about two months whether or not the mother breastfeeds. Prolactin interferes with the body's production of oestrogen and progesterone, keeping low the already depleted supply of these hormones.

Hormones are chemical messengers produced by the body and changes in hormones inevitably cause significant changes in mood and behaviour. It is almost certain that this hormonal upheaval plays a major role in the weepiness and emotional rollercoaster of the baby blues. It may also play a part in postnatal psychosis – though it is still unclear which hormones are involved and what they do.

Weaning is another difficult time. It's worth bearing in mind that as you stop breastfeeding, prolactin levels drop, causing a drop in the levels of endorphins, the naturally occurring body chemicals that produce a sense of well-being.

Women who suffer from pre-menstrual syndrome do not seem to be at a higher risk of developing postnatal depression. However, there is a subtle and so far little understood link between PMS and postnatal depression. It is clear that women who suffer postnatal depression have an increased risk of having PMS after the birth. Dr Katharina Dalton estimates there is a 90 per cent chance that a woman with no previous history of PMS who suffers postnatal depression will get PMS subsequently. American research suggests that women who become low and depressed should expect a worsening of symptoms at a regular time in the menstrual cycle, usually in the days before their period but during or after the period as well.

Thyroid imbalance

After childbirth, the level of hormones produced by the thyroid gland drops to a lower level than before the pregnancy. These hormones carry messages to the brain that regulate body functions such as temperature control and energy levels. A minority of women develop an underactive thyroid immediately after birth. The symptoms are sluggishness and exhaustion, along with weight gain, dry skin, constipation and mood swings. Some women with hypothyroidism, the medical name for the condition, may be mistakenly diagnosed as suffering from depression and given treatment accordingly. In fact, hypothyroidism is easily sorted out with hormone treatment. The first step is a blood test provided by your GP which can quickly and effectively distinguish between the two conditions.

Psychological factors

First-time mothers

'Oh, poor thing,' says Chris whenever she hears of someone being pregnant for the first time. 'I feel sorry for them in a way,' said one 65-year-old mother of eight at the news that her daughter was pregnant. Both were acknowledging that the first baby is not just a new beginning; it's also the end of an era. The arrival of the child marks not only the end of the pregnancy, but also the loss of the freedom of being childless, the loss of being the couple that fell in love and learnt to live together and the loss of the person you were before you had a baby. That is a lot for the first-time mother to cope with.

First-time mothers may also be more at risk of postnatal depression simply because they're more likely to have unrealistic expectations and an idealized picture of motherhood. Women today can go through the whole of their pre-motherhood lives without any experience of handling a baby beyond a cautious cuddle of a tiny, sweet bundle which can be handed over to the parent if it starts crying. We become so familiar with the 'Aaah' factor in response to babies that we expect to adore our own from the second it's born. We've heard about sleepless nights but we assume that they're few and far between. We're told by family, friends and medical professionals to relax and enjoy the baby, as if relaxation played the smallest part in the never-ending turmoil of early motherhood, the exhaustion, the night-time feeds, the painful breasts and sore nipples. And there are the emotional changes that follow from putting your child's needs first, turning your priorities upside-down and radically changing your relationships as a partner, daughter, friend and worker.

'I think that whatever anybody says about having children, you are never prepared for it,' confessed one woman to a researcher. 'I went to all the classes . . . you never saw any further than the birth. Everything is geared towards the birth. Then suddenly you are there with this helpless little thing with no instruction manual.' As psychologists Ann Dunnewold and Diane Sanford put it:

> *Being a mother is being in the trenches, mucking out the stalls, contributing much that is neither glorious nor immediately satis-fying. Parenting is tough work. If you know you're tackling a tough task and others around you agree that its a tough task and support you in your undertaking, you are less likely to feel badly if you stumble a bit along the way. If you expect something to be a breeze and it turns out to be a hurricane, you may begin to doubt your aptitude as a parent or to suspect that there is some-thing wrong with you.*

People we trust to tell us the truth don't always do so. Our own mothers who've been through the experiences have forgot-ten the horrors or prefer not to take a killjoy role. Teachers at antenatal classes prefer to avoid the negative aspects of preg-nancy and motherhood because they see their job as instilling confidence in their 'clients' – and perhaps also because they prefer to avoid facing their own fears. Our friends who've already given birth may be graphic about the details of the labour but reticent about the problems they faced thereafter. Western society makes quite harsh judgements about 'good' mothers and 'bad' mothers, and women who have problems with motherhood are not just seen as unfeminine or unnatural. Because of the type of publicity that postnatal depression attracts they may also be seen as dangerous or inadequate. Even if our friends do complain, we often choose to condemn them as moaners or lacking maternal fibre. Finding out the reality of the demands that will be made can cause anger, depression and self-doubt at just the time when those demands are hitting in. And by that time, we're often on our own.

Older mothers

In the UK, the average age for having a first baby has risen from 24 in 1971 to 28 in 1992 and has almost certainly gone up since then. Every year, thousands of women in their 30s or even their 40s become mothers for the first time. There are well-documented advantages. Older mothers are more likely to be better off financially, better established in their careers – and therefore probably less anxious about work – and, according to research, they are likely to have more intelligent offspring.

But there are a number of reasons why older mothers may also be more at risk of postnatal depression.

- They are more likely to have moved away from home and, perhaps for career reasons, may have moved several times. This makes it less likely that they live within a supportive community.

- They may find the loss of work identity more painful than they expected as they suddenly become just someone's mother or a housewife.

- They may have unrealistically high expectations of motherhood or, having waited so long for a baby, feel extra pressure to get things right.

- They have become accustomed to both the routine and the excitement of work, to choosing how to spend their time and money and to feeling in control of their lives. Such pleasures may seem small fry compared to the bond of motherhood but that will not necessarily reduce the disruption. Old habits die hard.

- They are more likely to have developed defences against difficult emotions such as depression as they've got older. These defences may not survive new parenthood. The vital necessity of apparently trivial treats such as lunching with friends or leisurely shopping sprees may only be missed once they're impossible to achieve. And headier pleasures such as competing with men in a man's world, scoring victories in office politics or enjoying the admiration of others may be more important to your self-esteem and feeling of competence than you realize until you've given it all up. Depression, anxiety or panic may suddenly have a free-for-all as the defences disappear.

Before the birth of her baby at 38, Kay's mother warned her that she had her life separated too neatly into little packages. 'It was true. I didn't realize how much I was used to doing things my way. I thought the only thing that would change would be sometimes having to get up at night. But I lost control over what I did almost entirely.'

- They are more likely to be in a relatively new relationship, with both partners accustomed to a career-orientated, 'wining and dining' lifestyle. That can deepen the contrast between life before and after the baby and make it more difficult to adjust.

'Tony and I married a year after we met and we had a baby almost straight away,' says Isabel, now 35 and mother of Jack, 18 months. 'We felt as though we'd known each other for ever. But somehow we couldn't pull together once the baby arrived. I'd want to go to bed once he got home from work. But I couldn't say that to him in case he was offended. There were things we couldn't take for granted.'

Perfectionists

Some women have high expectations of themselves and feel a huge sense of failure when they don't meet those high standards. Such women are setting themselves up to fail if they believe that they can do things perfectly at a time of enormous physical and emotional change. It's sometimes difficult to recognize perfectionism as a problem. If you feel anxious, panicky and depressed by your early tentative and imperfect steps and can't learn to laugh at yourself, you may develop a permanent sense of failure, undermining confidence and self-esteem. One reaction to this kind of self-doubt is to try and increase the amount of control over other parts of your life – cleaning the house obsessively so that you shine in its reflected glow or constantly demanding reassurance from your spouse, friends or health professionals.

'I remember my GP telling me at the six weeks check-up that my daughter Josephine was underweight. I was absolutely devastated. I couldn't bear the idea that I wasn't getting her feeding right or that she wasn't a perfect child. For ages I felt completely panicked. I couldn't talk about her weight and always changed the subject quickly whenever it came up. In retrospect, it would have been so easy to give her a supplementary bottle,' said Sally.

Keeping control

Antenatal classes and baby books are mostly concerned with helping mothers keep control during birth and early parenting. But new evidence suggests that trying to keep control of what are essentially uncontrollable events can lead to a lack of satisfaction and depression. Women who are encouraged to talk about their feelings, perhaps admitting that they did not maintain control during childbirth or are finding difficulty in coming to terms with being a parent are less likely to become depressed than women who bottle up negative feelings and resentments and try to maintain a façade of coping.

You can talk to your health visitor about these kind of feelings at any time. You may not be ready to talk about the birth straight after the event. Your health visitor will understand if you want to talk about such feelings weeks or even months later.

'Inherited' depression

Many women who develop postnatal depression have no previous history of psychological problems. However, if you tended to be depressed or anxious before becoming pregnant, you are clearly more vulnerable to depression once you have a baby. Depression in early life often relates to childhood experiences – and having a baby inevitably brings both women and men up against their own childhood experiences. We remember the good things about the way we were looked after by our parents – the childhood lullabies and stories pop into our mind and we find ourselves using the same affectionate names as our parents did. But if our childhoods were difficult, if we were neglected or the victims of emotional, physical or sexual abuse, we may feel undermined, lacking confidence and anxious about how we're going to react to our own children.

If you were a victim of abuse as a child, you may have already received help in the form of counselling or psychotherapy before deciding to have a baby. If difficult feelings surface only when a baby is born, it is important to seek help and be prepared to undergo therapy to help you to resolve your feelings as early as possible. If you do have thoughts about harming your child, remember that you're unlikely to act on them as long as you know there's a problem and are doing something about it.

There is no consensus on whether susceptibility to depression is genetic. But there is evidence that the children of depressives are more likely to suffer depression both in childhood and throughout life. Back in 1936 Anna Freud said: 'maternal depression at any point during the first two years may create a similar depressive mood in the child.'

Recently, Margaret Drabble recalled being so depressed at the age of nine or ten that she used to wish she could die in her sleep. While outwardly, she seemed to be going through a normal schooling, she was surfacing every morning 'to such anxiety, darkness and oppression that I could hardly believe I could endure the day.' Later in life, she realized that the cause was her own mother's depression. The child of depressed parents, she said, has 'no strong person to kick against, it dare not try to destroy the weak and depressed parent so it takes the suffering upon itself. The child feels protective, responsible, yet powerless: the infection takes before the child is old enough to develop resistance, and the depression is often linked to an unexpressed and inexpressible rage.' Having learnt now how to control her mood swings as an adult and as a highly successful writer, she cannot forgive. She recalls her mother greeting her 'as I took her morning tea in bed with a cloud of dark, infectious misery and I think, No, that was not good, that was not creative and was probably not even necessary.' The solution is to 'do our best to make sure that our sour grapes don't set our teeth on edge', otherwise 'the cycle of misery continues, the sense of failure is handed on like a baton'.

Unresolved losses

Losses need to be grieved over and the grief expressed. Otherwise they will rise up again at times of emotional weakness, such as around childbirth. There are many events which, if unresolved in your mind, can lead to postnatal depression – the loss of a parent or other loved one, perhaps close to the pregnancy and therefore almost ignored until after the birth, or the death of a previous baby either through stillbirth, miscarriage or abortion. It may be loss of a friend or loss of health or loss of security by moving to another town or even another house. The more significant the loss, the longer it takes to feel emotionally settled – unless the loss is faced and grieved over.

Unplanned or unwanted pregnancies

People who are flexible and open-minded tend to see change as an opportunity to grow as a person, are open to new experiences and are more likely to be emotionally stable. Such people see themselves as an important person, as important as their partner, their family and their workmates.

There are many reasons why an unwanted pregnancy remains unwanted after the birth but almost certainly the main ones are a lack of flexibility and a fear of change. This attitude may well be part of the syndrome of 'inherited' depression.

'I was in such a state that I shouted at my daughter: "I wish I'd never had you",' recalls Sarah. 'As I said it, I realized that my mother had said the same thing to me and that it had been inside me all those years.'

You may actually feel grief-stricken as a result of having a baby that, for some reason, you don't really want. It's better to face up to these feelings and talk about them to someone safe, perhaps a health visitor, or the unhappiness can stay with you.

Jennie developed pneumonia when her first child was two years old and believes it was because her immune system was as depressed as she was. 'After his first birthday, I began to feel I was losing control over my life. It was when Sam started crawling and then walking that all the negative feelings that I'd suppressed during the pregnancy, came back. When he was an infant in my arms, he was small enough for me still to feel as though my life was my own. But the growing child filled me with fear and apprehension about the future. With my second son, I became distressed at almost the same time. I became very restless, walking the street every evening when my husband came home sometimes with tears running down my face. I started shop-lifting. I was picking up things I didn't want without really trying to hide it. It wasn't surprising I was arrested. It wasn't until ages after when I was better and the boys were older enough for me to enjoy rather than fear them that I connected these two breakdowns with my very ambivalent feelings about both the births.'

Relationships

With your baby

Sleeplessness and the impact of prolonged sleep disruption cannot be underestimated and may be a far bigger cause of depression in both men and women than has been previously realized. Talk to your health visitor if your baby's crying at night is leaving you exhausted and unable to cope. There are now sleep clinics in most towns where expert and effective help is available.

Bonding – a mother's emotional response to her infant – is 'the dynamo which empowers her to maintain the never-ending vigilance and sustain the exhausting toil of the protection and nurture of the new-born,' says psychiatrist Ian Brockington. It is a strong, natural instinct that takes hold in the early days or hours of the baby's life and is rarely affected by emotional disturbances such as depression. However, one in two women who eventually bond with their baby, feel little or no warmth towards it for around six weeks and occasionally up to a year. It may cause concern and contribute to a feeling of depression. Bonding can be delayed for a number of reasons.

- Colic, a common disorder, probably caused by an under-developed digestive system in the baby, used to be considered a sign of inexpert and inconsistent handling – and these hurtful judgements are still made. It causes the baby to experience visible physical discomfort and means that it cannot easily be soothed. And whatever the cause, it can strain the mother's confidence in looking after the baby. A baby that smiles early and often is known to elicit earlier and deeper bonding with the mother. A colicky baby that screams every night can have the opposite effect.

- Mothers may also find it difficult to bond with premature babies and those who need surgery or hospitalization after the birth – particularly if they are not encouraged to stay with their baby during this difficult time.

Ellen's daughter was born six weeks prematurely and stayed in the special care baby unit for three weeks. 'No one talked to me sensibly about bonding and I was happy to go along with the people who told me to take advantage of that three weeks to get myself back into shape physically, relaxing in the knowledge that my baby was in safe, professional hands. Yes, I went to the hospital each day, but it was a lacklustre approach. Perhaps an hour or so peering at this tiny foreign being, a few minutes of cack-handed cuddling, or an attempt at a feed. It was not until my second child was born three years later that I realized what I had missed out on. The rush of love and closeness that comes with real bonding.'

- The shock of giving birth to a baby suffering from a disability or an abnormality can disrupt bonding, particularly if sensitive counselling is not available. Many parents find it impossible to see beyond the problem to the loving and loveable child.

Sandra, whose son was born with a club foot requiring repeated surgery from the first month of his life, recalls her failure to focus on him rather than his foot. 'I was going through the motions of caring for him, taking him in and out of hospital. But it didn't occur to me that we both needed kisses and cuddles. When we did finally bond, it was as though the sun had come out.'

George and Susan were told at a routine scan that there was something wrong with their baby. 'It looks like you're going to have a circus dwarf,' they were told. Both became deeply depressed during the first year of Sam's life. Susan came close to committing suicide and they considered separation. They were finally helped – by other achondroplastic dwarfs – to love, respect and enjoy their son. 'I'm angry at the way we were treated,' says George. 'The beginning of Sam's life could have been far more positive.'

- Some mothers and children are 'emotionally mismatched' – the parent perhaps quiet and introverted, the child loud and noisy. It helps to recognize any such mismatch rather than pretend it doesn't exist, and to accept the baby for its own personality. In one study, comparing a group of women who were depressed with a group that were not depressed, mothers who described their children as 'fussy, unadap-table and unpredictable' were five per cent more likely to be depressed.

With your partner

Depression inevitably has an effect on those around you. And irritability and resentment can lead to depression in one or both partners after the birth of a baby, particularly if neither of you are getting enough sleep. Even if you have an inkling of the numerous changes your relationship with your partner will be under, the enormity of these changes may shock and alarm you as you struggle to readjust, say American psychologists, Ann Dunnewold and Diane Sanford.

What happens is that the baby takes over your lives. You don't have time left for your partner, you don't communicate well because you're both stressed and exhausted and sex or a cuddle, once the best way to end a row, is now too much of an effort. There's so much more work to do. If your partner is out at work and you are at home, you may both be resentful at the supposed easiness of the other's day. It may seem to you that your partner has no idea what you're going through: endless hours, no breaks. At the same time your partner may feel resentful about working all day and then coming home to a wailing baby, dirty dishes, no dinner and you looking like the walking dead. If you both work, the stress can be even worse – with the evenings spent trying to unwind while looking after the baby.

New evidence shows that men are just as susceptible to post-natal depression as women. They may be already depressed as a result of unemployment and financial worries for instance, causing depression in their partner; they may become depressed as a reaction to the birth; or they become depressed as a reaction to their partner's unhappiness. The fact that a depressed parent gets 99 per cent of their care and support from their partner creates an inextricable emotional link that can cause a spiral of despair, sometimes leading to a breakdown in the relationship and separation.

With your mother

The psychotherapist Joan Raphael-Leff describes the moment of giving birth for the first time as being like a Russian doll – the birth marks the transition for a woman from being the child of her mother to being the mother of her own child. To mother generously, she says, a mother needs to feel mothered, and the absence of a loving mother to support her or enrich her from within can make her veer from trying to live up to an idealized idea of herself as the perfect mother she never had, to being a deprived daughter who feels a gap instead of maternal resources.

She quotes Kate, describing her own postnatal depression many years earlier, who said: 'When my baby didn't smile, I felt he was withholding from me. On the other hand, sometimes I resented him clinging to me and refusing to go to others. He just wanted me all the time. I felt smothered by more demands than I was capable of responding to. I needed someone to share it and to give to me as I was giving. Other people had their mothers but my mother was dead and my husband didn't really understand. I felt I was getting nothing good from anybody.'

It's relatively easy to bring about a painless, comfortable transition to motherhood when you have the luck to have a mother who is alive, accessible (though not necessarily round the corner) and when your relationship with her is healthy and relaxed. If your own mother is geographically or emotionally distant or, indeed, no longer alive, then it's harder to feel that the transition has really occurred and that you really are independent and mature. It's equally damaging if the mother is critical or over-intrusive. However much you may have achieved as an adult, and no matter how confident you may feel as a woman, pregnancy can push you back into ingrained childhood valuations – which may be more powerful than those you encounter in your daily life.

Psychologist Dorothy Rowe identifies a damaging pattern of behaviour in mothers whose own mothers were depressed.

> You will probably not want to imitate how your mother parented you but at times you may find yourself treating your child as your mother treated you. It is not that you intend to give your baby mixed messages or to be unloving, but these are the relationship patterns you learned.

She describes one woman who would stop speaking to her mother whenever they had a disagreement, sometimes for months.

Neither would forgive the other. Setting such an example to the children, the grandmother and mother ensured that the three daughters never got on well together. Even at their father's funeral two of the girls would not speak to one another and now one of the girls is completely estranged from the family.

Understanding this emotional transference, whether it's a cascade or a trickle, is the key to defeating its adverse effects. As Sylvia said: 'I used to be angry with my mother. Now I understand more about why I feel like I do and I'm angry with her mother, my grandmother.'

There may be harder emotions to deal with. You may find your own baby triggers memories of sibling rivalry of younger children, anxieties and secret destructive wishes against your mother's babies that may have left you feeling guilty and ineffectual. You may even envy your own child the love you yourself lavish on it while desperately wanting to be the perfect mother you wish you had. 'It seems to be the case that women who can remember a deprived or neglected childhood, do better,' says psychotherapist Dilys Daws. 'It's when your childhood is blotted out, that things are difficult. That's why talking about childhood is so important.'

With your friends

When Rachel had a baby, she was surprised when a friend observed that only women who had given up on being themselves had children. It is important to realize that friends who haven't got children don't necessarily stay around after a baby is born. Germaine Greer noted that as she became older she became invisible to people like waiters, who took far longer to serve her. The same can be true of friends when a woman becomes a mother. Remember that if your friends find you boring, it's time to find new friends.

There may be other reasons for a change in your circle of friends. You may have moved house to another town or district, perhaps to find a larger house in a more congenial area to bring

up children. Women who give up full-time work either permanently or to take maternity leave can also find themselves
suddenly isolated. In many ways, it's an ideal time to develop
new friendships with women who share motherhood and
the same kind of future if not the same past. But it's not
always easy.

Dorothy Rowe describes Jackie's story after her husband was
posted to another town when her son was three months old. 'I
became very lonely, no friends, no one to chat with, started
taking it out on Ron. Neil was not a sleeper, caused a lot of trouble at nights, I became over the next few months very nervous,
depressed, aggressive with Ron, I remember feeling very low at
the time, I went to the doctors with it but couldn't talk about it,
couldn't talk to Ron about it, couldn't talk to friends, couldn't
talk to Mum as she's the kind of person who says "I've had
seven kids I never felt anything like this, so it doesn't exist".' She
became deeply depressed, yet unable to ask for help and was
eventually admitted to a psychiatric hospital.

Excluding intimacy is dangerous. 'We must include some people
in a group with us for if we stay on our own for long enough we
become odd,' says psychologist Dorothy Rowe. 'I like my own
company and I really enjoy taking time off work to get on with
some writing in solitude but I am home only for a day or two
when I find that I am holding imaginary conversations out
loud.' We need other people, she says, 'to maintain our sense of
existence as a person, the arena in which you experience everything that happens in your life.'

When questioned, a high proportion of women with postnatal
depression have no one that they confide in or only one confidant. A study of women in Britain and in Greece asked
women whether they were able to identify with the following
statements:

- Even if my parents lived far away, I know that if I were in need, I would be able to depend on them.

- If I am upset or confused I know there is always someone I can turn to.

- There is always someone with whom I can share my happiness and excitement.

- I believe in times of difficulty my neighbours would help me.

It found that in both countries, the feeling of not having good support from friends, families and neighbours was a major predictor of postnatal depression.

Single parents

The stereotypical single mother is poverty-stricken, exhausted, lonely and full of regrets. But of course that is not necessarily the case. Today, a woman can choose to have a baby on her own knowing that she has adequate financial means, the self-reliance and the support of friends and family to take on the job with confidence – and that becoming a single parent is normal and acceptable.

However, single parents are more likely to have faced an inner struggle in the early months of pregnancy over whether to keep the baby. And a single mother is more likely to have to face the stress, fatigue, uncertainty and anxiety of motherhood on her own without another adult to provide reassurance, 'breaks, back rubs and breadwinning', as Joan Raphael-Leff puts it.

Once again, a woman who keeps a stiff upper lip, determined to put a brave face to the world and to 'do it all' is probably going to be more vulnerable to postnatal depression than one who admits their negative feelings of disappointment and grief at missing either a real person or the loss of an ideal, who reaches out to other people for help and accepts that as a human being as well as a parent, they need fun, satisfaction, companionship, entertainment and rest.

Loneliness

You don't have to be a single parent stuck in a high-rise flat to be lonely. What turns your fleeting feelings of loneliness into an illness is an absence of support, loving care and attention – an interest and focus on you as individual rather than as the role you are playing in being a mother. When Princess Diana gave her famous BBC TV *Panorama* interview, it was her declaration of marital infidelity that caught the headlines. But thousands of women responded to her courageous and moving account of postnatal depression. Despite the fact that she had beauty, adulation, wealth and youth, she also had many of the classic risk factors for the illness – a difficult pregnancy, major change in the year before the birth, a separation physically, and possibly emotionally, from her mother and, above all, a lack of support from those closest to her. 'You'd wake up in the morning feeling you didn't want to get out of bed, you felt misunderstood and just very, very low in yourself,' she explained. 'I never had a depression in my life. But when I analysed it I could see that the changes I'd made in the last year had all caught up with me and my body had said: "We want a rest". I received a great deal of treatment but I knew that what I needed was space and time to adapt to all the different roles that had come my way. In the space of a year my whole life had changed, turned upside-down and it had its wonderful moments but it also had challenging moments. Maybe I was the first person in this family who ever had a depression or was openly tearful. And obviously that was daunting because if you've never seen it before, how do you support it?'.

Conclusion

This chapter has described the risk factors that doctors and health visitors are trained to look out for when they monitor women during pregnancy and after the birth. But there are other factors that can interfere with our ability to develop as parents. These are covered in the next three chapters.

CHAPTER 3

The part professionals play

When we're ill, we look to professionals for help – but it has to be said that they haven't done spectacularly well in the past when it comes to postnatal depression. That's partly because of the nature of the condition, for although postnatal depression may become an illness it doesn't start off as one.

As a new parent you are more likely to develop depression if your normal responses to the inevitable changes in your life are condemned as dangerous and wrong, especially if you are encouraged to ignore or repress those responses. Unfortunately it is clear that some aspects of the hospital-based obstetric service that have developed in the West over the last 30 or 40 years have tended to exacerbate the problem by failing to allow time and space for the expression of anxieties. Health professionals have been trained to reassure their patients, rather than encourage them to talk about their concerns and worries.

When women become depressed, the professionals have sometimes failed to recognize the condition. And even when they have recognized it, they've been unable or even unwilling to offer therapeutic support. This is not a new scandal. Organizations such as the National Childbirth Trust have campaigned for years against what they see as the impersonal style of obstetric care in hospitals. And there has been recognition for nearly a decade that GPs, the first port of call for most depressed people seeking help, have been, for one reason or another, very poor at diagnosing clinical depression in general. There has been such concern about this that the Royal College of Psychiatrists and the Royal College of General Practitioners have been running a five-year campaign to raise awareness of the condition among professionals as well as the general public.

But the emotional problems around childbirth, it appears, have been a special area of neglect. In recent years experts from various specialties have looked at the kind of psychological support available to women in antenatal clinics, obstetric wards and postnatal check-ups and have come up with disturbing results.

In antenatal care

Some women are frustrated and discontented with the antenatal care available, particularly with antenatal clinics in hospital. Consultants are often rushed and impersonal and women feel they are on a conveyor belt of care. This is often a tragic missed opportunity. Psychoanalyst, Joan Raphael-Leff says a pregnant woman may be

> dying to listen to her child's heartbeat on the stethoscope yet too shy to ask for a go. She wants to hear from the busy midwife what it is like to watch a baby come out and how she thinks this baby is coming along but doesn't ask because time is short. She wants to talk and be recognised, to tell her version, to be asked to report her own internal experience of how each movement feels and tell them that she can now identify little limbs. Above all, she wants to be treated as an adult person on a creative mission, an active, cognisant participant in a strange exciting experience, not merely a dumb container come to the workshop for a service checkup.

Midwives and teachers in antenatal classes often do not 'include time for the expression of negative feelings, such as anxieties about the normality of the baby, still birth and their own physical integrity.' These anxieties range from concerns about the birth, being cut, stretched or torn, to whether their husbands' feelings will change after the birth. Women question their own capacity for maternal feelings and wonder if they are really mature enough to care for a child. They fear that if they can't put into practice all that they have been taught, the staff may react with impatience and they may 'fail'. Psychiatrists now say that women who face their fears before the birth, and above all talk about them and have these fears accepted as valid and reasonable, cope better afterwards. Yet the health professionals looking after them at this time have traditionally seen it as their duty to give reassurance – whether it's justified or not – and to play down negative feelings about the birth and parenthood.

Why? Gone are the days, thankfully, when the message in some antenatal care was that with the right breathing, childbirth can be pain free – that the pain of labour is the price that's paid for getting it wrong. Such an attitude is now rightly regarded as 'maternalistic' and just as harmful as heavy-handed paternalism. But the remnants of maternalistic midwifery in refusing women the opportunity to air their fears still prevail. Dilys Daws points out that almost all of us have been touched in some way by postnatal depression either directly in ourselves, in our mothers or daughters or friends or colleagues. Midwives and health visitors sometimes used to stifle discussion of negative feelings as much because they didn't want to face their own fears and anxieties about birth as because they saw their duty as instilling confidence.

In obstetric care

The importance of 'sensitive and individualized' care in the delivery room may be appreciated by every mother but it is not always put into practice by health professionals. In 1984, French obstetrician, Michel Odent found that women who were given 'sensitive and individualized' care in the delivery room were less likely to experience the baby blues. 'Although they became emotionally labile in the few days after delivery, it was described as a pleasurable release of feelings,' he reported.

Another research study found that in a Guatemalan hospital

which had added to the obstetric team non-professional women employed to provide mothering and support throughout the birth, women had fewer physical complications, shorter labours and greater emotional stability both immediately after the birth and later on.

Yet the West has been slow to take on board the implications of this kind of research. Why is this? One reason may be that it's part of Western medical training to adopt an impersonal attitude to the 'patient'. The medicalization of childbirth has been criticized for years as being peculiarly inappropriate – women giving birth are not sick. Yet attitudes have been slow to change. Midwives change shifts, student doctors practise their skills and other staff come and go with little acknowledgement of the private and disturbing nature of the birthing experience.

Only recently have midwives been taught communication skills as part of their core training. This is an essential addition to the midwife's range of skills. A woman in labour has a heightened awareness and is more aware of the tone of speech or a glance of disparagement or disapproval than of what is actually said. Some women may project on to the midwife or doctor feelings that arise from authority figures in their past, parents in particular. Women with domineering mothers may fear the same approach from the midwife; women with ineffectual mothers and caring fathers may put their confidence in the male doctor and see the midwife as inadequate. The midwife has a difficult task in that they have to give intensive, highly personal care to a woman they have only just met – and provide empathy and support to women who may even be hostile to them.

During postnatal care

The vast majority of cases of postnatal depression are not recognized by midwives, health visitors, GPs and obstetricians, even though they see the women regularly. Until recently, midwives and health visitors have not been trained in mental health problems and may well have been at a loss to know how to help even if they could recognize the signs. 'Their own feelings of ignorance and helplessness may even lead them to avoid the depressed mother,' says Dr Diana Riley.

Collusion between doctor and patient 'to keep the consultation as non-psychological as possible' has been described by another psychiatrist, Malcolm Goldberg. The patient doesn't want to run the risk of getting involved in stigmatizing psychiatric appointments, particularly as the mother of a small baby. And the doctor may be concerned that telling someone they are depressed can be a self-fulfilling prophecy. This is not true, he says. A 'respectable number' of people recover from depression just by having an appointment made to see the psychiatrist after an initial assessment interview. Having depressive feelings accepted as valid by a diagnosis of clinical depression actually makes the depressed person feel better. They have shared their distress with another person – which was what they needed to do.

A study of health visitors in Cambridge published in April 1996 showed that while health visitors were very good at spotting women facing the kind of problems that are caused by postnatal depression, they were very bad at identifying the illness behind the problems. They noticed, for instance, that certain women had 'significantly more difficult' babies than the mothers with good mental health, that these women were having 'significantly more problems' in coping with their babies than other mothers and yet did not ask for help as much. Yet these observations rarely prompted the health visitor to direct extra help towards these women. The women who got the most help and support were the women with good mental health, who knew what help they wanted and asked for it. Nearly half of the mothers who were actually suffering from severe depression and were being seen regularly by a health visitor were neither identified as being needy nor offered support.

It's well known that people who suffer from depression find it very difficult to ask for help. Even when they are aware that they are depressed, they may make an appointment to see their GP and then not turn up or, if they do, find that at the last minute they can't summon up the courage to voice their real fears and instead come up with a trivial complaint or talk about aches, pains and tiredness that are part of the depression. In new mothers, this pattern of behaviour leads thousands of women with postnatal depression to be dismissed by their GPs as hypochondriacs and time-wasters.

Medical attitudes are changing, but even now postnatal depression is often overlooked by GPs in favour of some physical diagnosis.

Seven weeks after delivery, Carol still felt constantly tired and physically drained even after sleeping, her limbs felt limp and shaky and she often had dizzy spells. 'My GP tested me for diabetes and thyroid imbalance but these proved to be negative. He then admitted that I was a puzzle to him but said that it would probably pass and I should just plod on'. After several months of 'plodding', Carol took a serious overdose and was admitted to a psychiatric hospital. This was followed by outpatients treatment and eventually she made a full recovery.

Even when GPs do recognize postnatal depression, they may not know how to treat it. Many do not know about counselling schemes or about the safety of antidepressants during breast-feeding. And the doctor may assume the condition is mild and short-term and therefore be reluctant to refer the mother to a psychiatrist, particularly as few have a special interest in postnatal depression.

The research

Highlighting these problems has helped make them out of date by provoking more research and attention to research results. In Britain, the obstetric service is becoming much more community orientated, and although more health visitors are needed, the profession is in the process of revolutionizing its care of women with postnatal depression.

A series of experiments carried out by psychiatrists, psychologists and health visitors from 1989 onwards helped to bring about this change of attitude. They were the first tests to measure changing mood during pregnancy and in the months after birth, made possible by the development of a questionnaire known as the Edinburgh Postnatal Depression Scale which extensive testing showed was a scientifically reliable method of identifying women vulnerable to postnatal depression.

In one study, a thousand women identified early in pregnancy as being vulnerable to depression were studied throughout their pregnancy and followed up after the birth. Half the women were given a number of 'interventions' aimed at protecting them against depression while the other half were given traditional antenatal and postnatal care.

The interventions worked. After the eight weeks, 69 per cent of at risk women in the intervention group were not depressed – but only 38 per cent of those who did not receive counselling had escaped depression. In other words, two thirds did not succumb to depression when they were provided with extra intervention compared to only one third without it. And there was one striking finding. Out of all the interventions that were provided for the women, one stood out as being particularly effective – talking. Women in the 'intervention' group diagnosed as suffering from postnatal depression by the psychiatrist on the study team were offered eight weeks of intensive counselling by a trained health visitor.

What became clear was that health professionals who already see new mothers regularly can be trained to identify and provide therapeutic support for women at risk of, or already suffering from, depression. The extra training involved learning to listen to the mother without jumping to conclusions or rushing to make judgements.

It was suggested by people like Dr Riley, that the intervention system should include certain key components:

CONTINUITY

If possible, a woman should see the same professional, probably the health visitor or community psychiatric nurse, throughout her pregnancy and through into the postnatal period. 'This will ensure continuity of care-giver during the often critical period after birth when women may be feeling particularly vulnerable,' reported psychologist Sarah Clement in a paper published in January 1995.

> To withdraw a supportive relationship at the end of pregnancy is unlikely to be beneficial and may leave women feeling abandoned at a time when they are likely to be in particular need of support. Postnatal 'listening visits' might also have an important debriefing role, allowing women to talk through events in labour and delivery helping to prevent feelings of post-traumatic stress following childbirth.

The importance of this continuity has not been lost on other professionals who are now busy turning the theory into practice. Dr Naran Harayan, an obstetrician at Leicester General Hospital, has joined a multidisciplinary working party involving the council, psychiatrists, health promotion experts, schools and self-help groups to support families through postnatal illness. 'What informed my decision to participate,' she says, 'was the frustration at losing touch with mothers sometimes within hours of sharing the experience of them giving birth. We're the people who've seen the woman through antenatal care and the delivery and it seems obvious that our role should not stop suddenly when the baby arrives.'

FORMAL GUIDELINES

The approach taken by health visitors during these listening visits follows carefully tested formal guidelines designed to give women 'permission to talk about their feelings and to disclose negative mood'. This is a crucial element because all the evidence shows that women with postnatal depression are ashamed of their emotions and do their best to hide them. Undoing these taboos requires careful, sensitive questioning.

A NON-MEDICAL APPROACH

Rather than trying to prevent postnatal depression or cure it, in the way that doctors approach clinical health problems, the aim is for health visitors to 'help people to find their own solutions and draw on and strengthen existing support systems'.

SUPPORT FOR THE PROFESSIONALS

This apparently simple therapeutic technique can actually be very stressful for the professional involved. It not only generates extra work, but, to be truly effective, the health visitor needs to listen to what a mother really feels about herself, her partner and the baby and what is disclosed can be quite shocking – anxiety, anger, self-hatred, hatred of the baby or partner, disturbing dreams, fear of damage that has, or might happen. 'Postnatal depression is painful to recognize,' says psychotherapist Dilys Daws:

> Those of us working with it professionally are likely to have been touched by it personally, as depressed parents or as the children of depressed mothers. Working on behalf of others is often reparative, a chance to put things right for ourselves vicariously as we help others. But thinking about the cause and effect of postnatal depression may be difficult to bear.

It is an essential requirement of listening therapy that a network of support is available for the professionals as well.

A new model of care

A new model of antenatal and postnatal care has been established and variations on the model are already being implemented in many parts of Britain. The proposals include the following.

Antenatal care

At the first antenatal visit, the health visitor provides the first active reflective listening. This is a meeting of perhaps an hour to establish a trusting relationship and to provide information about the realities of parenthood, including the possibility of low mood and where to get help, to discuss the role of the health visitor, to give information about sources of support in the area such as mother and toddler groups, baby sitting groups, and to provide leaflets about postnatal depression. Throughout the pregnancy, the health visitor continues to visit the woman, encouraging her to talk about herself and her feelings about the pregnancy, making it clear that she is there to support the woman and not just check up on the baby, and stressing the importance of the woman talking about her feelings to her partner, to a friend or to a professional. It is important to make it clear that she is being seen as an individual and that her wishes will be respected.

Antenatal clinics

Changing the ambience of antenatal clinics can make a difference. Simple measures such as providing tea, coffee and comfortable chairs transforms a sterile medical environment into a friendly meeting place. Newcomers to the area or women who have been at work and do not know their neighbours can get to know other new mothers and discuss their problems. It should also be a place where first-time parents can find explanatory leaflets and updated lists of local facilities for pregnant women and their partners. Parents or parents-to-be would also make use of a library. In one health education library in general practice, out of 400 books freely available in the waiting room for patients to dip into or borrow, books on mental health and childcare proved the most popular.

Parents say this kind of support gives them a feeling of being able to take control of their new lives rather than feeling ill-prepared for the reality of the baby's arrival. They feel that they've been 'empowered' to take control over their own lives. And women who are encouraged to realize the importance of confiding in their husbands and enlisting their support not only get more help from them, but are also less likely to become depressed. Couples who may have otherwise found their relationship under pressure as a result of having a baby are more likely to stay together and be happier together if they are given specific advice such as to:

- seek information and practical help as much as necessary;

- make friends with couples experienced in childcare;

- avoid moving house;

- get plenty of rest;

- discuss plans and worries;

- cut down on unnecessary activities;

- arrange baby-sitters.

The labour room

Doctors and midwives are now encouraged to implement the following guidelines during the delivery:

- Provide continuity of *empathic* care throughout labour and birth.

- Give parents 'centre-stage'. This is their day – but don't assume the father is providing emotional support.

- Be sensitively aware of the woman's on-going emotional state.

- Listen to the woman's stated needs, keep her fully informed and involve her in all decisions.

- Remember that women in childbirth have heightened perceptions and may remember a casual remark made by a carer. It is important and should be a matter of courtesy not to talk to colleagues about the woman or about anything else as if she wasn't there.

- If the woman seems to be losing control, help her to regain her sense of self.

- Help the woman to deal with pain by recognizing it as valid –

81

and not underestimating it as some midwives and obstetricians do. Provide information about pain relief, respecting her choice of what she wants but helping her to decide on alternatives if necessary and knowing the value of the emotional support they can provide.

- Don't intrude at the moment of creation – allow the parents time to be with each other and their infant.

After the birth

Women need rest and peace after the birth. They also need emotional support. Psychiatrists John Cox and Jeni Holden believe the health visitor has a key role to play in providing this support. 'Staffing levels should be sufficient to allow midwives or the health visitor to spend up to half an hour of quality listening time with each mother every day, ensuring that she is given explicit encouragement to talk fully about her feelings and her early response to mothering'. The question to ask, they say, is: 'The baby's fine but how are YOU?'

The guidelines for health visiting after the birth are as follows.

1. The health visitor provides a 'mother-oriented' rather than a 'baby-oriented' service so that the mother knows the extra attention is for her, rather than imagining that the health visitor is concerned about her ability to care for the baby.

2. The health visitor contracts to visit the mother for a set number of weeks at a pre-arranged time.

3. Having a regular weekly appointment means that the mother knows when her health visitor is coming and can prepare for the visit with things she wants to talk about.

4. Asking the woman to arrange for her baby and/or children to be cared for during this time not only assures the mother that she is being taken seriously but gives her 'permission' to ask for help from others.

5. The woman gains reassurance from knowing that she has support, that someone understands and that other people go through similar experiences.

6. The woman is encouraged to talk about her experiences in her own way without having to answer questions relating to the interviewer's agenda.

7. Talking about her feelings helps the woman to think more clearly about her situation and decide what she can do.

8. Not being given advice directly gives the woman confidence in her ability to make her own decisions.

What about men?

All this leaves one vital factor out of the equation – men. As the next chapter shows, this is an unfortunate omission which can and should be changed – and in some pioneering projects, it's already happening.

CHAPTER 4

Mother and father

Psychotherapist Malcolm Stern had been a counsellor for 13 years and happily married for six when he and his wife had their first child. It was a disaster. 'We stopped liking each other,' he says. 'I felt jealous of the attention Amanda was getting and she felt resentful that she wasn't supported enough. We both felt rejected. We spent a year not really talking, not having sex and making escape routes in our heads. I was thinking I could always go off to Kathmandu; she'd given the relationship a year.'

In an interview in the *Independent* newspaper, Malcolm Stern recalls the intense hatred that grew between himself and his wife as 'the images we had of each other collapsed and all we wanted to do was run away'. Amanda found Malcolm 'physically repulsive' while Malcolm 'decided Amanda was a professional victim'. 'It was not a comfortable place to be but underneath those thoughts was the real pain of not feeling cared for by each other.'

We never find out what happened to Snow White, Cinderella and the Sleeping Beauty when they got down to the business of marriage and babies with their handsome princes. But the implication is that the rapture of true love continues, while the girls raise cute kids and the princes ride their white stallions up and down, collecting the taxes that keep the next generation in sweetmeats and ballgowns. But it's not always like that – even for psychotherapists.

Marriage guidance organizations identify five areas of danger for couples who have become parents:

1. JEALOUSY

Two's company, three can be a crowd. James, 33, was so resentful of the new baby that he couldn't bear to see his wife, Helen, breastfeed: 'I felt my two-week old son was invading my territory and I couldn't make that feeling go away. I started to keep my distance which Helen noticed. When I tried to resume our sex life, she told me I must be joking.'

2. LOSS OF INTEREST IN SEX

Research shows that most couples get back to the sexual relationship they had before the pregnancy within a year of the birth. But before then, many women are actively hostile to the idea of sex. It's not just that they're tired. If you have spent the whole day feeding, holding, cuddling, rocking and carrying your baby, you may have fulfilled your need for physical contact and closeness. By the end of the day, you don't want to be touched or fondled – you want space around you in bed and you want sleep. Unfortunately, as a result, your relationship loses a valuable resource. Kissing and cuddling is the way couples often put a row behind them. If that's not happening, then rows might not be ended so easily.

3. RESENTMENT OVER HOUSEHOLD CHORES AND CHILDCARE

Women at home with a new baby can be so exhausted that getting dressed is an effort. Yet the partner who is going out to work all day feels he needs sleep because, after all, he's the breadwinner. Night-time feeds can be a cause of potentially long-lasting resentment. Even if she is breastfeeding and therefore primarily responsible for actually feeding the baby, a mother may feel that her husband could at least get up and settle the baby back in its cot – if only to show willing.

And it's not just the feeding. There are a range of childcare responsibilities, ranging from who changes the nappies to who takes time off work when the child is ill, which have to be either shared or done by one person. Ordinary household tasks may be up for negotiation: Who cooks the dinner? Who goes to the supermarket? Who empties the rubbish and sees to the washing?

'We argued about who was going to do everything from making tea to hoovering,' says Kate. 'I was the one that had extra work from the baby so it was right that he should do far more of the housework than me. But he saw me at home all day and insisted that it was my job. Neither of us dared compromise because so much was potentially at stake.'

4. CHANGES IN PRIORITIES

Before Phillip and Jane's baby was born, they were both career-minded. That all changed when the baby arrived. While Jane was preoccupied with motherhood, Phillip was mostly interested in his imminent promotion prospects and that's what he wanted to talk about when he and Jane were together. Jane said, 'We no longer seem to be on the same wavelength. Then when I told Phillip that I didn't want to go back to work at all, he was furious with me.' Phillip's version of the episode is different. 'I couldn't tell Jane but I was completely taken aback by her change from career woman to full-time mother. I was terrified at the prospect of being the family's sole breadwinner and I suppose I was obsessed by the need to earn more money.'

5. RESENTMENT OVER MONEY

For couples whose views on budgeting, spending and saving differ, there can be a huge escalation in conflict once a baby arrives. Even if a woman is only stopping work for a short time, either unpaid or on paid maternity leave, she is likely to have to rely on her partner more. Those who've given up work entirely have to get used to asking their partner for money. Suddenly having only one income instead of two can cause panic, and it is worth remembering that the impact of losing your independence, however generous and open-handed your partner, can be far greater than anticipated.

⊷ ⊷ ⊷

'We'd never had a row about money and he wasn't mean,' recalls Karen. 'We'd moved to the country to have the baby

and suddenly I was completely dependent on him for everything. It was an enormous change and I felt as though I was
always on my guard for a look or sign that he resented me. I
suppose I felt a bit guilty that he was out there flogging his
guts out and never had anything to show for it.'

For Janice, money worries became serious once she'd had the
baby. 'Money was always something that slipped through my
partner's fingers. When I had my own income, it didn't really
matter. He was the one who paid for treats and I paid the
bills. I assumed he'd do both when I stopped work. I don't
think we ever really discussed it. But he didn't change. I was
dependent on him and he was undependable. I hated it and
I hated him.'

There are good reasons for organizations to single out these
five areas of concern. Becoming a parent is widely seen as an
immensely satisfying, joyful event that cements a relationship
by offering the opportunity for 'normal adult personality
growth and change'. The Victorian-style family with the breadwinning, authoritative paterfamilias and the loving, submissive
mother continued well into the second half of the twentieth
century. But it's perhaps no coincidence that the divorce rate is
rocketing as the gender roles have become blurred – with the
transition to parenthood often becoming the flashpoint. Most
divorces occur in the first four years of marriage. There are no
statistics collected on how soon divorce follows becoming a
parent. Anecdotal evidence suggests that one in ten couples
have 'significantly weakened' marriages by 12 months after the
birth of a child, and seven out of ten husbands feel they have
drifted apart from their wives during the first year after the birth
of a baby.

Until recently, about as much was known about the mechanics
of relationship break-up following childbirth as about the post-
marital fate of fairytale heroes and heroines – surprising, perhaps,
in view of the persistent interest of media and politicians in the

break-up of the family, the destruction of family values and the damage done to children by divorce or being raised by a single parent. There are three areas in which the lack of interest, support and information are particularly pronounced.

1. MEN'S ROLE IN REPRODUCTION

Birds do it, bees do it – and it's normally the male of the species that takes the more active role. But once the deed is done, it's the woman who is in the spotlight. She's the one that changes shape, gets backache and morning sickness, is ritually monitored by white-coated health professionals, gives birth, breastfeeds and establishes the primary bond with the new baby. Men's role in all this is passive and voluntary. Most men choose not to go to antenatal classes or medical appointments, and though most do attend labour nowadays, it is not always clear exactly what they are supposed to do while they are there. Many men feel superfluous. They may become emotionally upset and have to be supported by staff as much as their wives. Perhaps even worse, some men protect themselves against their own anxiety by developing an interest in the technological equipment, aligning themselves with male doctors or taking on the role of mediator between the woman in labour and the staff, interpreting procedures and describing what is happening.

After the birth, the gender differences continue. Women's active role in reproduction means that the huge emotional changes involved in becoming a parent are easier to make. 'When a woman becomes a mother, she has her own mother as a role model and then experiences a series of physical changes that happen gradually yet inevitably,' says Kate McKenna, who is a multidisciplinary co-ordinator of services for postnatal depression in Leicester. 'We like to think that men readily accept parenthood. Yet they have to make a great leap on their own to become a father and it's even more difficult for them to become an involved and caring father.'

Men today are less likely than women to have handled babies before they have their own – boys don't usually get to baby-sit either for siblings or for friends and neighbours. 'We assume that women have an instinctive understanding of their baby which they don't always have. But almost all men are unsure about becoming a father,' says Carmel Spreadborough, who specializes in postnatal depression for the mother's support group Meet-a-Mum. 'You do occasionally meet mothers who haven't a clue about their baby's basic needs – they don't know how to hold it or they expect it to talk straight away, for instance. But fathers can be far more ignorant and there's less urgency or opportunity for them to voice their concern and ask for help.'

Men's uncertainty, their not knowing what to do, may get in the way of their feeling connected to their new-born. Many men are afraid of intruding on their wife's relationship with the baby say American psychologists Ann Dunnewold and Diane Sanford. They may have received messages from their own father, from society and even from their partner which reinforce the feeling that it's not 'manly' to get over-involved with the care and nurture of children. 'After all *real men* don't wear aprons and they certainly don't push vacuum cleaners with a baby on their hip.' The result is that one year after the birth, 40 per cent of fathers have never or have rarely changed their baby's nappy and fewer have ever bathed the child. Many uninvolved fathers are out at work or enjoying hobbies or leisure at bath-time of course – but it may be deliberate avoidance and this may actually be a sign of the father's distress.

It is part of the same picture that health care workers have routinely ignored men in the preparation for the birth and in the support provided afterwards. The message at the end of the twentieth century is that having a baby is still women's business – and although men can tag along, they are essentially superfluous.

2. UNDERSTANDING EACH OTHER'S NEEDS

What women want from their men and what men think they want are often very different things, according to new work from London University's Men's Studies Research Group. Pregnant women want emotional support, the feeling that their partner is tuned in to their needs and expectations. Expectant fathers, on the other hand, tend to be acutely aware that more will be needed of them as a parent and often see their ability to provide practical support as a priority. Having taken on to build an extension, make a cradle or take on overtime, they may be surprised when their partners are resentful rather than grateful. After the birth of the baby, these different priorities can become even more polarized and misunderstandings can develop rapidly and dramatically.

Textbooks on postnatal depression list 'unsupportive partners' as being a risk factor for the illness. But it's probably more correct to talk about 'unsupportive relationships'. Women suffering postnatal depression are likely to be over-critical of their partners, with the irritation frequently centring on the man's lack of involvement in the care of the baby. But the research suggests that men's lack of involvement is often a symptom of the man's lack of confidence as a parent, a lack of confidence which his partner may help to foster.

Because he is not the main participant, the man depends on his partner to reassure him that he is a competent father. If that reassurance is lacking, as is often the case when the woman is suffering from postnatal depression, his confidence in himself and her confidence in him can spiral downwards. 'The partner may want to do the right thing but he's walking a tightrope and he may not get it right whatever he says,' says Carmel Spreadborough. 'I've spoken to thousands of women with post-natal depression and so often they say to me: "My husband doesn't understand. He's horrible to me", while the husband will be telling his story in another way: "It's nag, nag, nag from her now. There's no pleasing her."'

And he may well be right. He may try to show love and affection but be rebuffed by a woman for whom hugs mean sex which will interfere with sleep. He may respond with hostility himself and by doing so provoke more hostility from her and a literally vicious circle of anger and resentment can be established. If he responds by withdrawing from engaging in the argument, he may well still be perceived as aggressive by his partner. The couple may simply stop talking to each other. Or the man may use 'the male strategy of self-distraction', sometimes destructively if, for instance, he increases his alcohol consumption to dangerous limits – go into any pub and the men sitting sadly at the bar pouring down pints are likely to be newish fathers. Or he may find himself as the target of attacks from an intolerant partner who feels increasingly that her own expectations, whether unrealistic or not, are being ignored. Home becomes the focus of negative emotions, hostility, anger, mistrust, with both partners feeling far easier and relaxed with strangers and acquaintances than they do with each other. 'I remember the moment when I realized that I was safer, happier and more comfortable outside the home than in it and it was then that I decided that I was going to seek a divorce,' recalls Janice.

3. INSIGHT INTO MALE DEPRESSION

Fashions in behaviour come and go. But it seems unlikely that the brief enthusiasm for 'New Man', before he was replaced by the all-farting, boozing, football-mad 'New Lad', will return quickly. According to women's magazines, New Men who talk about their feelings and cry are boring and unsexy. Women, it seems, don't want men feeling sorry for themselves and this is especially true when they become fathers and, as such, are expected to take on the role of protectors and providers. 'Social expectations of men and male gender too often preclude men from feeling able to disclose personal concerns,' says Malcolm George of the Men's Studies Research Unit, to such an extent

that they may experience rejection if they do attempt to admit concerns or weaknesses to others. Many men are aware of this constraint and obedient to it but it can be an oppressive burden. The price for a man of not coping or being 'depressed' can be the justified fear of being labelled uncaring, unsupportive, selfish or unmanly, pathetic.

Yet by not addressing their emotional needs, men put themselves at risk of depression, divorce, separation from their children, illness and suicide.

There is clear evidence today that it is perfectly normal for men to go through the same emotional rollercoaster as women after having a baby. The man's depression may not always be a result of becoming enmeshed in his partner's feelings. The man may already be depressed as a result of factors external to the relationship, such as unemployment, or the birth of his child may bring up problems related to his own childhood. Just as women who find motherhood difficult have often had a difficult relationship with their mother, so men who have a poor relationship with their children have frequently had a distant or inadequate father.

Whatever the reason, these normal, though turbulent emotional reactions are bearable only if they are recognized, understood and talked about. And it is essential to make sure that they are. A lack of understanding, communication and mutual support quickly becomes a crisis once a baby arrives. Depression is now thought to play a major role in family violence and family dysfunction, whether it surfaces as postnatal depression or not. Depressed patients often report their close relationships as marked by high levels of conflict. And there is also evidence that child abuse, including infanticide, is more likely to occur in families where one or both parents are depressed.

What can be done?

There is a new recognition that men should be as closely involved in antenatal and postnatal care as possible. In the United States, a campaign has been launched to inform men about emotional illness after childbirth and to encourage them to seek help if their wives develop postnatal depression. A pamphlet handed out at an American West Coast postnatal class entitled 'HEY, FATHERS-TO-BE, HEAR-YE' warns men that their wives are at risk of 'Princess Di's Disease' in the form of a wife who's 'grumpy, irritable, hostile, 3 x gravity exhausted, not sleeping (and for sure not with you). One hour she may appear near normal and the next, "What do you mean, where did I buy this pretty outfit? I haven't had anything new for a year while you squander money on your toys in the garage every week".'

The pamphlet warns that this kind of behaviour has a terrible effect on men. 'You will feel infantalized, angry, confused, ashamed, helpless, hopeless, guilty and frustrated. "What did I do to get this?", your temporal limbic left brain will be asking. Before when I got this hostile treatment, I really fouled up or did some heinous act. I've done nothing for the past three months but play nurse and cook meals.' Its advice is for men to recognize that they have 'the only rational brain in the family. ... No matter how hostile or impossible she and your marriage has become, persevere until you get help for this formerly lovable and now unlovable woman. This is too often the beginning of divorce.'

In Britain, Mel Parr, a counselling psychologist working in the field for 20 years, has developed an alternative programme to support men and women throughout the transition to parenthood. It's not yet widely available but is influencing other practitioners in this area.

Her views on what parents need at this time can be summarized as follows:

• Men and women have an equal need for support from the beginning of pregnancy through the first months of having a child.

• Their needs at that time are for emotional support rather than the sort of practical medical advice on preparing for birth and childcare that are the stock of antenatal and postnatal care today and which is widely available in baby books, videos and magazines.

• Most new parents need help and not just those who seem at risk of depression. This may be a modern problem. In the days when families were bigger and more tightly knit, people learnt from watching older siblings' experience of having children and absorbing the fact that becoming a parent is not a single crisis but a series of complicated adjustments.

• Silence is not golden. Couples benefit from learning to communicate their feelings rather than bottling them up, however difficult they this may seem.

- Antenatal classes teach women how to take control of birth and the care of their new baby. But this is not necessarily helpful. In fact, parents benefit from being helped to recognize that childbirth and early parenting are essentially uncontrollable events – and that the least exhausting way of coping may be one of 'learned helplessness'.

- Feeling that you have to be positive about childbirth and parenting can actually increase dissatisfaction and depression. If you're told repeatedly that everything will be all right, it's more difficult to admit that things actually aren't all right – even, or perhaps particularly, to your partner. Both men and women may fear that the relationship may not survive talking about difficult emotions. Though men, in particular, may seem unfazed by the changes brought about by a new baby and more concerned with work than their role as fathers, they may be concealing bitter feelings of rejection or loss of the woman who was their sexual partner. Couples may appear to be coping well but below the surface are repressed differences and disagreements which eventually take their toll.

'Our research shows that it is almost inevitable for couples to come under pressure when they have a baby, especially the first baby,' says Mel Parr. 'A vital part of the transition is that the couple have to grow apart and change their relationship to make space for the baby. It's not always easy to do so.'

Her research has convinced her that what new parents need is help and encouragement to acquire good basic communication skills so that they can talk calmly about negative as well as positive emotions, air conflicts and listen to each others' complaints. As a result, they may argue more than people who bottle up negative feelings, but in the end, they're more likely to be able to agree to disagree and to feel that their beliefs and emotions have been aired, acknowledged and listened to with respect.

Take, for example, sex – a frequent cause of conflict. Many new mothers lose interest in sex – a fact normally blamed on the woman's fatigue and pelvic discomfort. It may actually be a biological constraint, a hangover from primitive times when to survive in the first year a baby needed its mother's full attention, undiluted by romantic diversions or a subsequent pregnancy.

A couple able to engage in 'constructive conflict' will be able to talk about the woman's conflicting roles of mother and lover, argue about it, reach some form of understanding and stay close as a couple, even if not sexually. A couple that has got into a habit of avoiding conflict may simply not mention the problem, while she is worrying about it and he is resenting it. A couple able to engage only in 'destructive conflict' may try to explain the way they feel – but it'll soon become a complaint and end up as a slanging match.

The same applies to other issues. Women who are encouraged to voice their feelings and concerns are less controlling in their attitude towards the baby's crying or colic. They are more likely to understand that a baby's antisocial behaviour is not naughtiness but its way of communicating a need. Men who are given the support don't necessarily become more involved as fathers, but they're more likely to believe that a very young infant can communicate and develop a relationship with its father and to be more tolerant of the baby's behaviour.

Details about PIPPIN, the organization Mel Parr set up in 1994 to further this work and to train facilitators, can be found at the back of this book.

Conclusion

At no time are we more aware of being animals than during the process of reproduction. Yet we fail to take account of a number of behaviour patterns that are part and parcel of normal reproduction and assume that having a baby in the 1990s has somehow been tamed. Unanticipated things that are, nevertheless, very likely to occur to a couple expecting a baby include the following.

- The woman may well expect the man to be especially strong and providing during this time – and, just as importantly, to put that commitment into words. She may be upset if he can't or won't demonstrate emotional solidarity with the mother-to-be.

- Many women go off sex in the months or the year after the baby's birth. Nature doesn't recognize contraceptives and takes over in the interests of the baby's survival.

- The division of responsibilities between a man and a woman becomes more distinct and may become a major source of conflict. Silence is not golden in this situation. Not talking about feelings can be almost as destructive as throwing tantrums and vases. TV soaps regularly show the most unlikely people sitting down and voicing their feelings or listening to their partners' complaints. Let them be your guide.

CHAPTER 5

Mother and baby, mother and work

Along with the baby booties, the soft toys and the cute outfits, there's one thing new parents can be sure of receiving – and that's advice. Anyone and everyone who has had a baby considers themselves an expert on the subject, including mother-in-law, granny, best friend's sister and the check-out lady at the supermarket. They all have their own pet theories about how it should be done and where 'bad' parents go wrong. And those are just the amateurs. The 'experts' can be even more demoralizing. There are the doctors and other health professionals who examine the new product at the baby clinic. There are the writers of baby care books and the psychological theorists who, from Freud onwards, have warned parents of the dire consequences to the child's well-being of being 'bad' parents.

Much of the advice can be seen as laughable, at least in hindsight. As psychoanalyst Joan Raphael-Leff points out, a British Medical Association manual on pregnancy published as recently as 1973 advises women to keep themselves 'regular', adding, without specifying any reasons, that: 'Attention to your appearance and hygiene in your pregnancy is very important, so make a special point of keeping yourself well-groomed, well-washed and sweet-smelling.' Two years later, a book by a leading obstetrician warned 'suggestible' pregnant women readers against old wives' tales but then went on to forbid them to cross their legs during pregnancy!

Nevertheless, the fact that we receive conflicting and sometimes laughable advice from experts doesn't mean it can be ignored. Pregnant women, anxious to do the best for their baby, clutch at straws and in their 'ignorance' and uncertainty doctors take on the role of witch doctor, says Professor Raphael-Leff.

The combination of the woman's unquestioning trust and the professional's empty reassurances or unexplained advice results in activities becoming unconsciously rooted in sympathetic magic (taking iron or eating sweet and wholesome things to produce a 'good' or 'strong' baby) while other instructions to relax, read a good book or take care of her appearance, seem to indicate that such activities will enhance the baby's appreciation of beauty and culture.

And parents are also sitting ducks for the politicians, columnists and pundits for whom they are there to be judged and frequently condemned as over-permissive, over-strict, irresponsible, over-protective or just plain inadequate. Fathers who abandon their families by walking out are condemned as irresponsible – though fathers who abandon their families for work, most days for most of the time, tend to get away scot-free. Working mothers or worse, career mothers (i.e. successful working mothers), get the brunt of the attack. As late as the 1980s, the bulk of research assumed that the employment of the mother and the use of shared childcare was disruptive to the family and damaging to the baby and viewed working mothers as 'deviant'. Even in the 1990s, when at least half of women with children under five go back to work, women are criticized for abandoning their vulnerable children to pursue their narcissistic, self-centred glory – though mothers who stay at home, at least when they are unsupported, are also condemned as work-shy layabouts expecting the State to pick up the tab for their children.

Almost all advice handed out to new parents uses words like 'ought', 'should', 'duty', 'normal' and, quite often, 'sacrifice'. There is an assumption that parents, and especially mothers, need to follow certain rules for the benefit of the baby – or risk disaster.

These approaches almost certainly represent a crass simplification. New research suggests that the mental health of the infant is closely linked to the mental health of the parent. In other words, a happy, relaxed, mentally robust mother or father will have happy, relaxed, mentally robust children. It's the sad, anxious, unconfident parent (possibly in this situation because her contentment and confidence have been undermined by the proscriptions of those in authority) whose children have problems.

It would be clearly absurd to equate the early return to work of new mothers with happiness and relaxation. Most women who return to work within the first six months of the birth, whether or not they are looking forward to going back, feel enormous distress on leaving their child with someone else, often describing their feelings as similar to a bereavement. And being a working mother, especially of one or more young children is exhausting and disruptive, both physically and emotionally. At the same time, there is a considerable body of evidence showing that women who want to go back to work yet stay at home out of a sense of duty, are highly vulnerable to depression. Psychologist Mel Parr, whose work on the transition to parenthood for men and women is described in the previous chapter, concludes that: 'In the 1990s, how women manage to balance work and home seems to be the criterion by which women judge their effectiveness as a mother.'

So what are the needs of new mothers and their babies? The phrase 'good-enough mothering' was first used in 1971 by psychoanalyst and paediatrician, Donald Winnicott. It does not, as is sometimes thought, mean that in childcare 'anything goes'. His view was that in order to develop normally, a baby needs to be cared for by the same person or the same small number of people during the first year of its life. The main function in these early months is for the adult, almost always the mother, to mirror back the baby's feelings and her own enjoyment of mothering so that the child searching the mother's face can come to see and value him- or herself. And by sensitively responding and being attuned to the baby's emotional cues and signals, the mother helps the baby to learn cause and effect – that when they cry, for instance, their needs will be met. As the baby gradually becomes more independent during the first year of life and the mother slowly resumes her own non-mothering activities and ceases to adapt herself entirely to the baby's needs, the child becomes aware of its dependence on her and begins to understand the difference between 'me' and 'not me' in an emotionally significant way.

Images of mother and baby have traditionally shown them engrossed in looking at each other. Recently researchers using video techniques have been able to analyse the vital importance of this time spent together. They have shown in convincing detail how mothers mirror the expression on their babies' faces. Babies seeing their mother's expression, know what the feeling inside them looks like. By two months, mother and baby, looking at each other, can talk to each other. The mother speaks; the baby replies with sounds or simply mouthing. Remarkably, they take turns and the rhythm is of a conversation'.

Mel Parr's research suggests that when fathers are encouraged to believe that a very young infant can communicate with and develop a relationship with their father as well as their mother, they find it much easier to develop a relationship as an individual from birth.

However, when the mother or father is depressed, these conversations go wrong, inevitably affecting the infant's behaviour. In a series of tests in 1991, researchers changed the normal looking-at and response between mother and baby so that the timing was out of skew. In the first test, the mother became still and expressionless for a period of 45 seconds, while continuing to look at her baby. The baby responded, typically, by protesting and then withdrawing, with its gaze averted from the mother's face. In the second, more complicated test, the timing of the mother's acts in relation to the infant was changed using closed circuit television. Mother and infant each saw a full-face life-size video image of the other so that they could establish eye-to-eye contact. When the images were relayed in real or 'live' time, the two were able to interact in a normal, mutually responsive way. But when the mother's image was delayed by an interval of 30 seconds, the interaction was disturbed. The infant was seeing and hearing the same maternal behaviour that occurred during the live sequence but 30 seconds later at a time when the mother's expression was no longer related to her infant's behaviour. The result was that the baby became disturbed, puzzled and confused.

When a woman is suffering from depression after the birth of her baby, she is far more likely to get her signals wrong. Being preoccupied with her own unhappiness, she may gaze at the baby with a blank face or mis-time her reactions. The baby then misses out on the life-enhancing two-way 'conversation'.

This leads on to a related area of difficulty for mother and baby. The most noticeable difference between a mother in good mental health and a mother with postnatal depression is that the latter is more likely to have 'significantly more problems in coping' with a baby who is 'significantly more difficult'. For when a baby loses its mother's attention, research shows that its reaction is to devise some kind of behaviour to deal with this.

- The baby may give up trying to get her attention and withdraw. The attempts at conversation stop and the mother and baby lose touch with each other. And because they are out of touch with each other, sleep rhythms and feeding can be disrupted, as can the early learning schedule.

- The baby may try to stay close to the depressed mother by imitating and identifying with the mother's mood. Research shows that when an infant imitates the mother's expression, it probably starts to feel what she feels. This means that one consequence of postnatal depression can be depression in the baby.

- The baby may try to cheer the mother up. This strategy often works when the mother is not too depressed, but it can happen that a very depressed mother responds with anger to the smiles and gurgles of her infant because they are so clearly out of tune with her mood. This can lead to an active baby becoming a hyper-active toddler, sometimes resulting in the label 'attention deficit disorder'.

This research has proved to be highly controversial. Many experts believe that except in cases of severe depression children are not necessarily affected by a short-term depression in the parent. There is also the fear that such research may induce guilt in men or women who have experienced depression during the early years of their child's life and who have to live with the knowledge of having taken something valuable from their children that they can never give back. Some experts regard the issue as such a hot potato that they are reluctant to speak out on it. In an article in the *Daily Telegraph*, a psychiatrist only agreed to talk about recent research suggesting that at four years, the children of women who have suffered postnatal depression may have impaired intellectual development, on condition that she would not be named.

Other experts, however, feel that there are three reasons why it is helpful for parents to be aware of research that pinpoints so eloquently the needs of a baby in its first year of life.

1. By understanding the significance of the adult/baby 'conversations' in the early months, a couple where the mother isn't up to the task for whatever reason, can make an arrangement for another adult, perhaps the father, to spend more time with the baby, getting to know it by gazing into its face.

2. Instead of feeling guilty about past negligence, it can be helpful and supportive for parents of a growing child to be aware that, as a baby, the child missed out on an opportunity to feel comfortable with itself and other people. There is no reason why the child's experience along the line cannot make up for this.

3. Knowing that the priority is to feel happy and relaxed rather than to do things correctly or incorrectly, should be a huge relief for new parents.

Back to work?

The early relationship between parent and child, and particularly mother and child, is special and should be given special thought, according to child psychotherapist Dilys Daws. This is especially important in an age in which so many women take as active a role in the world outside the home as men have always done.

A mother and baby find it easier to get to know each other if they exist, at least in the early months, in a timeless zone, she says.

> *A mother and baby relationship is not to do with the time-related achievement or productivity that we consider as being important in our everyday lives. Of course there are certain tasks that need to be carried out every day. But the important part of the way a mother and baby develop their understanding of each other has to be in a different time and space. It can't be done if you're giving a baby 'quality time' or 'token time'. The important work is achieved during the kind of time you spend day-dreaming or staying in bed in the morning or being in love. Being close to the baby at least in the early days means that somehow you have to feel that there is a value in hours, days, weeks, months of what may seem from the outside very much like wasting time.*

She is concerned that women who have tied themselves into a pre-set date to return to work are less able to get emotionally close to their baby, something that happens increasingly where there are financial penalties if an agreement over maternity leave is not honoured.

> *It's this business of timelessness. It does seem that it's more diffi-cult, for instance, to get feeding established when the woman knows that there are not endless weeks of reverie ahead, when she feels that there are other pressures that have to be considered apart from the need for both mother and baby to go at their own pace. I am not suggesting there is any 'ought' or 'ought not' involved or that women should feel obliged to give up a part of their life for their baby's well-being. But it may be that from a purely selfish point of view women may decide that they would be happier and more relaxed if they stayed at home for a while on an open-ended basis with their baby. And it may be that in the short-term as well as the long term that may lead to a happier baby who is easier to look after.*

Many women, she says, feel they must keep working not just because of financial imperatives but also because of a fear that as a stay-at-home mother, they may lose their edge in the outside world. 'The fear is that you might become a vegetable,' she says.

> And it's true, you do become a vegetable. That's almost the point of being a mother. You have to shed the high-powered focus, the rushing about, the cleaning the house in 15 minutes, getting to work on time, competing and achieving, and devoting leisure hours to ordered events in gyms and wine-bars. Doing nothing, or at least doing nothing as viewed from the outside world, is time-intensive.
>
> When talking to some working mothers in therapy, I often get the sense that they only have so much creative excitement and that by the time a woman gets home from a busy day in the office, she may have used most of it up. And the baby may well be aware of this, aware of the mother dressing up to go out, aware that the exciting part of the day is outside the home.

She is not, she says, talking about sacrificing yourself to your children.

> It's important to say that because many women who devote themselves to careers may well have an urgent underlying need to defend themselves against self-sacrifice, perhaps because they want to differentiate themselves from their own mothers who they saw as over-submissive and draining of their energy. On the contrary, I'm keen to alert women to the possibility that by going back to work too early, they may be sacrificing themselves in another way, sacrificing their happiness and enjoyment of life.

It's not the same for everyone

Most babycare experts seem to assume that the parent–child relationship is unique and always the same, a constant factor that is either improved or damaged by the way the parent, usually the mother, responds to the offspring. But we all know that isn't so. As psychologist Dorothy Rowe points out:

> *Some mothers love their child from the moment it stirs in the womb while others feel no more than a benign interest in the child for its entire life. Some fathers would lay down their lives for their children while others can desert the family home without a backward glance. Some children can never in their whole lives think of their parents without feeling a warming of their hearts while others cling to their parents only as a means of satisfying a need and discard their parents as soon as a more satisfying source becomes available.*

From the time we first make friends at school and visit other people's homes, we know that all mothers are not the same. There are huge differences in the way women organize their homes, their children, their own lives. Though all parents do the same things – we all hold our babies, feed, change and bathe them, are woken at night by an appeal for comfort, milk and winding – how we do it differs enormously. We may feed our babies on demand or try to stick to a routine. Some of us carry them around in our arms or a sling by day and keep them in our bedrooms at night, while others seem more comfortable picking them up only to feed, burp and comfort them. Some mothers find it easiest to keep their baby in their bed at night, while others prefer to leave the baby to cry itself to sleep on its own.

We tend to think that we are doing these things correctly or incorrectly according to which babycare book we've read. But the influential psychoanalyst Joan Raphael-Leff has shown that the way we look after our children is based on 'an elaborate idea of the kind of parent we wish to be and a set of beliefs of what babies are like', established before the baby is born, derived largely from our own experience of childhood – but also influenced by current factors such as financial pressures, size of the family and availability of childcare.

In her book *Pregnancy: The Inside Story*, Professor Raphael-Leff describes models of mothering and fathering which, she says, are deeply ingrained in the unconscious. They exist as impulses rather than as rational thoughts – but ignoring them or trying to do something that doesn't come naturally because you think it's the 'right' thing to do, is a type of behaviour that puts you at risk of unhappiness and depression. She quotes one unhappy mother as confiding: 'When my baby cries at night, my heart pounds and I feel this strange sense of anxiety, a real fear of death. Although my mother never admitted it, I think I've always known she was gripped by panic under all that false calm.' Another recalls her grandmother telling her that 'she would sit with tears rolling down her cheeks as she watched the clock until the next decreed four hourly scheduled feeding.'

'Parents can only do what they are comfortable with,' says Professor Raphael-Leff. 'And furthermore babies have an uncanny ability to detect fraudulence: people who in adulthood blame their parents for their misery seem more likely to come to terms with an authentic parent, however lacking, than with a deceptive one, however well-meaning.'

She describes three models of parental orientation. It is rare for anyone to be a pure example of one of these models; however those who form the extreme poles of each category tend to fail to recognize the child as an individual, seeing him or her only as part of the parental predetermined image. We are mostly a mix of orientations. It's helpful to be aware of the dominant beliefs underpinning our approach to parenting so that we can be ourselves without feeling guilty about it.

1. *The Facilitator mother* 'approaches motherhood as a long-awaited, deeply gratifying experience'. She feels that by carrying the baby in her womb, she has established a special understanding with it. Once born, she feels strongly that she alone has the intuitive capacity to interpret the baby's needs. She sees her role as adapting to the baby whom she believes knows best what it needs and communicates those needs non-verbally. It means the mother has to stay physically close to the baby at all times in order to decipher its needs. Accordingly, she:

   • breastfeeds on demand for as long as the baby wishes to suck day and night;

- keeps the baby in her arms or in a baby-sling for most of the day;
- keeps the baby in her room or bed at nights – which can involve her in frequent interruptions to her sleep whenever the baby makes a noise as it wakes in response to the sound of her stirring or the smell of her milk;
- feels bound to deny any ambivalent feelings about either her baby or her role as mother. She 'idealises her gratified baby and herself as bountiful mother'.

2. *The Regulator mother* sees maternal devotion as 'an over-rated myth propagated by society to keep mothers at home'. She is determined to get back to her 'real' life as soon as possible and insists on the baby adapting to her schedule. This mother:

- sees mothering as an acquired skill rather than something inborn;
- believes it's wrong to give her child the impression that she is the exclusive source of comfort and presents it with a variety of 'co-carers';
- believes her basic task is to socialize the baby, regularizing the baby's impulses, and so sets up a routine from the beginning, feeding at regular intervals, introducing supplementary bottles to enable others to feed and, if breast-feeding, plans to wean when the baby starts taking solids;
- feels that, because she achieves a predictable routine, she can leave the baby on its own – in a carry-cot, bouncy-chair or pram by day and in a cot in its own bedroom at night from an early age.

3. *The Reciprocator mother* appears to be somewhere in between these two groups but also has a specific philosophy of her own. Rather than seeing the baby as entirely merged with and dependent on the mother like the Facilitator, or separate and in need of socializing like the Regulator, the Reciprocator regards her baby as a person sharing similar emotions to herself and assumes that both baby and parent must learn to understand each other. So this mother:

- feels that the baby's needs are entitled to full consideration but so are everyone else's;
- makes special concessions to the baby's inability to wait to be fed, as well as its limitations in communicating and understanding language – although this does not mean the baby's needs always come first;
- is prepared to make continual adjustments to daily routines and activities to take account of the baby's changing moods and needs – as well the changing moods and needs of the household and other members of the family;
- is able to accept both the baby's good and bad aspects. 'My baby is wonderful and I love her,' says a typical Reciprocator mother. 'But when she wakes me for the umpteenth time, I could strangle her.'

In addition, there are similar orientations relating to fatherhood. For example, there are *Participators* who want to get involved in looking after the baby and *Renouncers* who don't. Once again, these approaches to parenthood are equally valuable in themselves as long as they are not carried to extremes – although there can be conflict when the father's approach to parenting doesn't mesh with the mother's approach.

1. *The Participator father*, as his name suggests, wishes to participate as much as possible in looking after the baby. He cradles, croons, strokes and caresses the new-born, taking over most of the baby care. This works fine when he is partnered with a Regulator mother, though if he has a Facilitator partner, he may be competing with her, possibly even participating in an undignified tussle over the baby's affections: 'Who do you love best, Mummy or Daddy?'

2. *The Renouncer father* is comfortable with a division of labour by gender and wishes to have as little to do with nurturing the young baby as possible. That pleases a Facilitator mother but could be very annoying to the Regulator mother who expects the father to relieve her of some childcare duties or at least to agree to pay for a childminder so she can go back to work or

resume social activities. Although preferring to be on the emotional sidelines, some Renouncer men may find the sight of their wife feeding or cuddling the baby disturbing. 'He treated my breastfeeding as if I was committing incest or adultery,' complained one mother of her Renouncer husband. 'I've had to give up nightfeeding altogether and just feed during the day when he's not around. It feels furtive.'

Obstacles to fulfilling parental orientations can cause depression. The Facilitator mother may open herself to depression if circumstances make it impossible to sustain the belief that her baby and her experience of being a mother are nothing less than perfect. 'When Jason cries, it tears me apart deep inside because I can't give him what he really wants,' admits one Facilitator mother. 'My placenta wasn't good enough to nourish him until term and he was born early before his liver could cope so he was jaundiced. I felt I'd ruined him. I wanted to give him everything to make up for it and wept such bitter tears over his first bottle after my milk dried up.'

There is also pressure on her because she has to:

- continually reject any feelings of envy, rivalry, irritation, depression or aggression towards the baby;

- suspend self-interest, personal needs and non-maternal adult interests;

- face increasing difficulty, as the baby grows, to foster the illusion that she and the baby cannot lead separate lives.

The greatest hardship for a Facilitator is to have to return to work in the early months of the baby's life as separation, and what she sees as abandonment, fly in the face of her very being.

On the other hand, the Regulator mother sets herself up for depression if she:

- feels deeply that inappropriate behaviour on the part of the baby shows her up as an incompetent mother;

- finds that the baby's 'raw needs and primitive emotions' erode defences that she has erected with her hard-earned adult competence;

- fears that in her effort to make her 'naughty' baby 'good' she may lose control and become potentially violent;

- has to maintain rigid defences and therefore prevents herself from becoming emotionally involved with her baby.

For some Regulator mothers, the hardship lies in staying at home when she would prefer to return to work – either because she thinks it is her duty to do so or because she is married to a Renouncer husband who insists that she stays at home. 'When I'm stuck at home with the screeching baby, I feel I'm going crazy and don't know who I am anymore or what he wants from me or how long I can stand his clinging dependence without throwing him out of the window,' one Regulator mother confessed to her therapist.

Many women, says Professor Raphael-Leff, experience internal conflicts between these two orientations, causing immense distress. 'I feel I'm not allowed to be a real person,' says one of her patients whom she describes as having a 'Regulator internal mother' criticizing her constantly for not being tough enough and a 'Facilitator conscience' that pricks her for not being sufficiently devoted. This leaves her unable either to regain her sense of self or find a way to meet her own, as well as the baby's needs. 'I'm supposed to be totally devoted but when I'm with him I'm always wishing I was somewhere else or that he'd go to sleep and not need me. Its unbearable for me because all the things I depend on to feel my usual self like reading and sleeping and keeping myself looking trim and well-dressed are incompatible with being a full-time mother.'

Today, an increasing number of women are Reciprocators. This approach to parenting flourishes with the increased awareness of the capacities – and the rights – of newborn babies. According to Professor Raphael-Leff there are less negative consequences to being a Reciprocator. Unlike Facilitators or Regulators,

Reciprocator parents don't have definite expectations of the baby and are thus less likely to be disappointed and distressed when the baby and parenthood fail to live up to parental hopes. The Reciprocator awaits the unfolding of the baby's personality and is protected from disappointment by this relative lack of expectation. But it means, she says, that such parents 'struggle daily with the paradoxical dilemma that granting rights to one member of the carer–baby tandem means the other is entitled too.' And by being open to change and adaptation in response to the needs of both herself, her family and her baby means that a mother will have to live with complex and often ambivalent feelings.

The above examples are all taken from Joan Raphael-Leff's book, *Pregnancy: The Inside Story,* but most of us can surely recognize versions of these categories and the conflicts that they can cause either in ourselves, in friends or in work colleagues. In a recent article in the *Guardian,* journalist Rebecca Abrams wrote that before she became a mother she assumed maternity leave would be something she would endure and that she'd be desperate to start work again.

> *But the first day I left my six month old daughter with a child-minder was like amputating a limb. I came home and sobbed. This can't be natural, I thought, this can't be right. Even now, I have the residual low-level fears that my daughter does miss out in some way by not spending more time at home with me. She is affectionate, curious, talkative, she loves the woman who cares for her and is loved in return. She is happy to go there in the morning, happy to see me in the evening. I carry on working and I hope for the best.*

Abrams wrote this account in response to a political campaign against 'irresponsible' working mothers to show how very seriously working mothers take their responsiblities. But the piece also shows just how much guilt-inducing conflict working mothers experience – conflict that may well be better understood, if not necessarily more easily borne, by Raphael-Leff's insights.

Conclusion

Babies need intensive parenting in the first year of life. The biological model is for the mother to devote the early months almost entirely to the new baby, nurturing its sense of identity and its understanding of the world around. But in the 1990s, good-enough parenting can involve the mother returning to work in the first year. The mother who returns to work should expect to experience a deep emotional reaction to leaving her baby with another person, both in herself and in her baby. But for the baby at least, this need only be temporary. Research shows that babies can have an intimate relationship with more than one person. So a mother can settle a baby with a carer, preferably one with the time and inclination to 'mother' a small baby, knowing that it will soon settle and by so doing, will enlarge its circle of trust. She can also rest assured that because the baby can 'bond' with more than one person, there is no need for her to feel her place in the baby's affections is being usurped. 'I've got to go back to work, I've got no choice if we're going to stay living here,' says Teresa, mother of a four month old boy. 'I just have to tell myself that it'll be a wrench, that it'll upset him a lot but that it will sort itself out in the end.'

Most women do have a choice about working, though one option obviously involves a cut in living standards. But if a woman feels very strongly that it is right for her to stay at home with the baby, there is no reason to assume that she is then giving up a working life. Motherhood, says Dilys Daws, is not necessarily a negative career move because it can help a woman to develop and become more mature – and therefore, arguably, more valuable in the workplace. 'The process of bringing up a baby requires as many negotiating skills as do board room deals,' she says.

With a new baby, you have to work out when it's going to be fed, how they are going to learn to feed themselves when they're weaned, when they're going to sleep, how they're going to behave – it's very complex and women, even when they've had children before, find themselves on a steep learning curve. It may be that women who hand over those responsibilities very early, may miss out on the opportunity to learn very useful skills. I always think of Mrs Thatcher who went back to read for the bar a few days after her twins were born. It may be that that's where her well-documented deficiencies in negotiating with other people, stem from.

CHAPTER 6

What support helps?

To come to the decision that you need outside help for depression is always difficult. With postnatal depression, that decision is even more difficult for a number of reasons:

- Everything is changing anyway with the arrival of the new baby, making depression even more difficult than usual to recognize.

- Postnatal depression can quickly become a way of life so that you cannot imagine a life in which you do not feel persistently exhausted, angry, resentful and lethargic.

- You may fear that you will be dismissed as a bad mother or even risk having your child taken away if you confess to being 'mentally ill'.

- You may feel that, even though you know you are ill, you will be a better person if you struggle on and beat the depression on your own.

- You may believe, as do many people, that the therapies and drugs available to treat depression, even if not actively damaging, are not helpful, at least on their own. 'I received a great deal of treatment,' Princess Diana said sadly in her *Panorama* interview, the brief phrase speaking volumes for the lack of loving care, attention and support that she really needed in her life.

It is important to remember the point made in Chapter 3, that professional help is not always guaranteed to be effective. Nor, unfortunately, will appropriate services always be available. However, if it is available, sensitive and effective professional support can offer a new start to parents suffering from depression. Most importantly it can offer them the opportunity to look at their life and see more clearly where changes are needed. When should you look for that help?

It may be that the realization that you need help will come to you or your partner in a blinding flash. Like Jessamy's mother, Susanna, you may find yourself changing a screaming baby's nappy and hear yourself say: 'I hate this baby!'. Or you may be like Ruth, who found herself crying helplessly one day at the prospect of a close friend coming round to visit – 'and a little voice somewhere at the back of my head was saying: "Hang on a minute, this just isn't me".' American psychologists Ann Dunnewold and Diane Sanford have drawn up the following guidelines to help you decide whether professional help is the best option going.

1. You know something's wrong but you can't get on top of it. You simply feel that you need a different perspective to turn things round.

2. You fear that you may harm yourself, the baby or any other person.

3. You are unable to sleep for more than three to four hours for several nights in a row or have other sleeping problems.

4. You have no interest in eating or it makes you feel sick.

5. You are unable to take care of the baby or yourself in terms of getting dressed, keeping clean and tidy and eating.

6. You feel speeded up or out of touch with reality.

7. Someone close to you tells you that it's essential to get help.

8. You are having panic attacks or anxiety symptoms which interfere with your daily activities.

9. You are experiencing persistent symptoms such as crying, anger, fatigue or hopelessness which are preventing you from running your life as you would like to.

10. Your baby is now at least six weeks old and your symptoms are not lifting but are staying the same or getting worse.

Once the decision to seek help is made, the next step is to consider where to go for help. A family doctor who knows you well and is also aware of the options for further care available locally is probably the first stop. Counselling is an important option, provided the counsellor has training and experience in dealing with postnatal depression. You may be prescribed anti-depressants or possibly even hormone therapy. Yet there is now a growing consensus that you may benefit from all of these therapies – and the best therapy is a mix of counselling, self-education and drugs. Here's why.

Talking therapies

There is nothing magic about talking to a professional. Anyone who is both understanding and caring will do, be they friend, mother or spouse. But it's not always easy to reveal our inner-most thoughts to our nearest and dearest at the best of times. Those close to us may not be very good at listening or we may simply have had little practise in talking about feelings. And in any case, the emotions that surface in postnatal depression are often seen as shameful and taboo. 'This is the great benefit of talking to a professional counsellor or therapist,' says psychotherapist Dilys Daws.

> It is extremely therapeutic simply to be able to talk about all your feelings to someone who isn't shocked by them, to put into words the terrible fears you have about what might happen to your baby, the terrifying dreams you have been having, the feelings of utter helplessness and hopelessness. Even severe depression can be enormously eased simply by having someone else know about the worst of what you are feeling.

It is also recognized that professionals such as health visitors or counsellors can act in *loco parentis* in a very special way during postnatal depression. Women with postnatal depression tend to see themselves as deficient, inadequate and worthless. Their distorted view of the world means that they interpret all events in a negative way, even when there is evidence to the contrary. A depressed woman will see a baby crying as a bitter condemnation of her mothering ability but she will ignore the times that the baby is contented and smiling. If her husband is angry with her, it's because of her rather than the fact that he's had a bad day at the office. And because she feels so worthless and inadequate, there is little motivation to change things because it's inevitable that whatever she tries to do, she will fail.

'A supportive mother doesn't just pass on her expertise, she tells her daughter how well she is doing, congratulates her on the good things she is achieving and celebrates them with her. That's very important to new mothers,' says Dilys Daws.

It seems that a friend or someone of the same age providing that kind of moral support, may not be the same. Often it is someone who is clearly older and wiser. It doesn't have to be the mother. It can be a mother-in-law or a motherly neighbour. But if there's no-one like that around, then a professional is probably the next best thing. Even if they are not older, a health visitor or counsellor can act in an older way, take on the role of a wise woman.

This kind of professional support, she says, may work best when it is provided regularly at a specific time so that the new mother can prepare the problems she wants help with, whether they are the baby crying, sleepless nights or her own emotions – and then having talked them through, take the solutions back into her life, knowing that that's not the end of it, that it's an on-going process.

There are a number of different therapies available. It's important to find someone you like and trust and who is also properly trained and experienced in treating postnatal depression. By the end of the first session, you should feel that together you have established an agenda for the therapy to progress and that he or she is going to be able to guide you in a positive direction.

Even if you do not get help directly from your health visitor, it is worth discussing the options with her. The different types of therapy available include the following.

COUNSELLING

This may be available at your local general practice or health centre. Your GP may refer you to a counsellor at the same time as prescribing antidepressant drugs. The evidence shows that even a short course of six to ten weekly sessions can help to beat depression. A good counsellor never judges or gives advice but listens carefully and sensitively, reflecting back a picture of what has happened to you throughout your life and what is happening to you now. This is the basis of counselling but it is especially important if you've got postnatal depression.

What's needed is a health care *partner* who can support and foster your own resources and help you to gain the confidence to take charge of your own recovery. There are different approaches to counselling. Some counsellors, trained in what is known as 'problem-focused therapy' will take the view that if you are suffering from postnatal depression you need a here-and-now approach, dealing only with immediate daily concerns, such as your feelings towards your baby or your partner, your lack of sleep or your panic attacks. They consider that it is only when you can get to a comfortable level of functioning that you will have the space and the desire to proceed to the underlying issues such as your early childhood, your relationship with your parents or your dreams. Other counsellors take the view that it's more helpful to confront all kinds of problems at the same time. It's worth considering which approach might be more helpful to you.

COGNITIVE THERAPY

This is a specific type of therapy which is widely considered to be particularly useful in treating postnatal depression. It may be provided by a counsellor, a health visitor, a psychologist, a community psychiatric nurse or a psychiatrist. The aim of cognitive therapy is to deal with here-and-now problems by changing the negative thought processes that underpin the depression. The aim is to help you to spot the negative thought patterns and replace them with more effective, positive approaches. You may be encouraged to keep a diary, noting the negative thoughts and the situations that set them off.

✎ ✎ ✎

Lucy was helped to beat postnatal depression after her therapist handed her a simple handheld clicking monitor that runners use to count the number of laps they have covered. 'I was instructed to click each time I had a negative thought and each time to ask myself – "What is the evidence for this? Is there another way of looking at it? Is it really as bad as I think?" Within a few days, I got very good at spotting the negative and replacing it with a positive thought. It really helped my confidence. And it was good to see my daily scores going steadily down as I changed the way I thought about myself.'

✎ ✎ ✎

PSYCHOTHERAPY

Psychotherapy is often regarded as an expensive option for the self-obsessed. But it may be of enormous value in combating postnatal depression, particularly for women in Western cultures where, as psychoanalyst Joan Raphael-Leff points out, 'there is little recognition of the emotional upheavals and birth fears or fantasies which are ritually catered to and ceremonially dispelled in other places.'

The time of giving birth, she says, is a time of heightened awareness of the mother or father's relationship with his or her own parents, whether dead or alive. 'Close-range, unremitting exposure to an infant for whom one has life-and-death responsibility evokes echoes of an inside story, powerful narratives and primitive, inchoate memories from a time when the parent him- or herself was a helpless child at the mercy of a seemingly omnipotent mother or father.' If there are unhappy memories of an abusive infancy, for instance, then the cycle of 'emotional and sexual abuse, neglect and violence may be perpetuated, as each successive generation is drawn unerringly and unconsciously to project, repeat and physically enact crucial emotional climates and relationships, actualizing and inflicting these on those closest to them.'

Psychotherapy, she says, is the best way to stop dead the cascade of abuse and bad parenting, the lack of self-esteem and confidence that can be passed on from parent to child. 'There is always a mythical parent whose perfection we fail to achieve. But we can only be ourselves – knowing our weaknesses, building on our strengths, we can try to avoid repeating errors by understanding them rather than burying them.'

By attending sessions once or twice a week, with or without your partner, you can internalize new insights and apply them to practical daily issues in the family between sessions. You will find that by talking out one problem, other problems, which have been lurking at a subconscious level, will emerge. These can then be resolved. The new insights resulting from this further resolution of emotional turmoil can also be gradually integrated into your life.

In *Pregnancy: The Inside Story*, Joan Raphael-Leff describes the case of Melinda, aged 32, who was referred for psychotherapy eleven weeks into her pregnancy because she was severely depressed. She couldn't stop crying, woke early and then stayed in bed all day instead of going out to work as a receptionist. 'In the early sessions, she was very tearful, usually arrived late, looking dishevelled and feeling exhausted. She felt herself to be a terrible person, totally unworthy of respect and thinking the therapist was watching her critically'. Gradually it emerged that she could not bear to contemplate becoming a mother or imagine the baby inside. Underlying this unhappiness about her new role was deep guilt about an abortion she had had in her late teens which, though it had seemed 'the only sensible solution to an impossible situation' at the time, had come back to haunt her with a vengeance when at 28, she found herself unable to conceive in marriage.

Further revelations occurred. Her mother had suffered a miscarriage when Melinda was young, an event closely followed by the death of her mother's father. The new baby boy born soon afterwards became the mother's favourite. As Professor Raphael-Leff says, 'Gradually a picture was drawn of an inhibitedly jealous and contrite little girl, always on her best behaviour, striving desperately to please and feeling abandoned by her cool mother who overtly preferred her son, whom she breastfed "constantly", to both daughter and husband.' It emerged that she had felt sorry for both her parents, particularly her father who she saw as abandoned by her detached mother. She tried 'but felt unable to win his affections although he was attentive when she was unhappy.'

Eventually she was able to acknowledge that her teenage fling with a married man had 'enacted her Oedipal desires as well as being an abortive bid for freedom from the oppressive home atmosphere and a search for the paternal as well as maternal love she craved' and to understand that 'the dynamics in her family of origin had kept her embroiled in her parents' lives rather than fully living her own.' Melinda, says Professor Raphael-Leff, was at last able to experience her long-stifled rage and sadness at the wasted years and saw for the first time 'that her own needs interlocked unhealthily with those of her long-suffering, silently critical husband who had grown up in a household with a depressed mother whom he had ineffectively protected from his violent stepfather'. She became robust and 'able to counter his doom-laden sense of imminent disaster with a new feeling of optimism.'

After the birth, psychotherapy continued, and when Aidan was seven months old, Melinda established a baby-sitting arrangement with another mother so that she could undertake professional training. At this time, 'Melinda's sexuality came back into focus in the sessions with emphasis on difficulties relating to sexual enjoyment and her overweight body. The work continued . . . .'

You may be able to be referred to a psychotherapist on the NHS either in the adult mental health services or at your local child and family consultation service. Your GP or health visitor will be able to tell you about this. But if not, paying to attend weekly or twice weekly sessions during the crucial months may well be an excellent investment. To find a local psychotherapist, write to the British Association of Psychotherapists, 37 Mapesbury Road, London NW2 4HJ. They will put you in touch with an assessor in your area who will then refer you to a psychotherapist if it is appropriate for your needs.

Drug therapy

Mood-changing drugs have got a very bad name. The tranquillizer scandal of recent years, during which over-prescription left thousands of people, particularly women, stranded in an addiction which was desperately difficult to throw off, saw to that. Many people still wrongly believe that antidepressants are addictive or even linked with suicide or murder. In the United States, depression has begun to lose its stigma, largely because of the arrival of new antidepressants such as Prozac, which, despite some claims that they can be dangerous, are widely seen as safe and effective. Six million people in the US take the drug, which is prescribed at the rate of one million scripts a month. Depression is now something people talk about openly and it's widely seen as 'the common cold of mental experience'. There are even jokes about it. A *New Yorker* magazine cartoon depicted Karl Marx on Prozac, declaring: 'Sure! Capitalism can work out its kinks'.

In Britain, depression is still a taboo subject even though it is both common – about one in three of us suffer from it at some time in our lives – and debilitating. Few people cite depression as a reason for sick leave. Antidepressants are regarded at best as a temporary sop and, at worst, a kind of mind control, stopping us feeling the pain of existence, and preventing us from reacting to the problems in our lives.

∿ ∿ ∿

Pauline suffered deep depression after the birth of her son eight years ago and she never really got over it. She had a painful pregnancy which left her not caring whether her son lived or died. He was a sickly child who did indeed nearly die in a flu epidemic and who was 'always troublesome'. She suffered repeated setbacks including having to escape from a violent partner and having to abandon her home and all her possessions. 'My child changed my life,' she says. 'Before he was born, my life was good. I was busy, fulfilled, popular, out seven nights a week. Since he arrived, it's been a mess. I suppose there's been good times but they've never been all that good. It just seems to have been grey all the time and I can't see much hope for the future.'

A series of doctors have recommended antidepressants for Pauline. But she has always refused and still cannot contemplate the prospect of having her life turned round by a bottle of chemicals. 'I just don't want that stuff pumped into my body. I've read too many bad things about it and known too many people who've suffered on it. I know they're not addictive. I know they're not like tranquillizers. But I want to rebuild my life on solid foundations not on something drug companies make profits out of. It would do me no good nor my child.'

Pauline's attitude to antidepressants is by no means unusual – 92 per cent of people in a recent MORI poll said that if depressed, they would prefer to have counselling rather than drugs. This is despite the efforts of the Royal College of Psychiatrists, which over the last few years has mounted a high-profile 'Defeat Depression Campaign' aimed at removing the stigma of depression and persuading a sceptical public that antidepressants, particularly the modern SSRIs (selective serotonin reuptake inhibitors), are both extremely safe with few side-effects, and effective.

What makes the message difficult to put across is that no one completely understands the physical processes causing depression, nor the way in which antidepressants work. Like much of medicine, they were discovered in a fairly hit and miss way.

Many of the antidepressants now on the market are derivatives of a drug originally used to treat tuberculosis in the 1950s. It was only prescribed as an antidepressant when doctors noticed that it caused extreme liveliness in recovered TB patients. One famous news picture from the 1950s shows inmates of a sanatorium dancing, smiling and clapping, with the caption: 'A few months ago, only the sound of TB victims coughing their lives away could be heard here.'

Scientists believe that depression is an illness with a physiological cause and that antidepressants can correct it by restoring the balance of chemicals in the brain, just as insulin corrects the imbalance that causes diabetes. Mood is determined in the brain by complex chemicals called biogenic amines. These act as transmitters, allowing communication between nerve cells. If biogenic amines are in short supply, for whatever reason, the communication between nerve cells is poorer and the mood of the person is lower. Older antidepressants, called tricyclics, work by slowing the complex process by which biogenic amines are destroyed once their job has been done, thereby boosting levels of the chemicals at work in the brain. Unfortunately, however, they work on a number of different chemicals as well so that most of these older antidepressants produce unwanted side-effects, including weight gain, tiredness and difficulty in concentrating – not exactly what you need when you are recovering from depression.

The newer SSRIs were the first antidepressants to be made from scratch using state-of-the-art animal and cellular models, and drawing on the skills of scientists from different disciplines. Though they work on the same principle, they are selective, working specifically on serotonin, the biogenic amine which regulates depression. They are therefore much cleaner drugs with far fewer side-effects – though some people do suffer increased anxiety on some SSRIs and there is concern that some, including Prozac, can also cause sexual dysfunction.

The impact of the SSRIs, at least in the United States, has been enormous as their lack of side-effects makes them far more suitable for treating people who are depressed. 'Psychoanalysts almost never prescribed antidepressants before Prozac,' says Peter Kramer in his book, *Listening to Prozac*.

Merely listing the side effects of the tricyclics interfered too much with the analysis. Patients would accuse them of hostility, of unconsciously wanting to poison them. If they did take the medicine, patients would spend long sessions on the couch complaining about how the analyst had made them constipated.

SSRIs do not interfere with the psychotherapeutic relationship in the same way. They are safe in the hands of potentially suicidal people (whereas tricyclics can be fatal in overdose), and they do not make people feel drugged in the way tricyclics did. 'Because both patients and doctors were comfortable with Prozac's side effect profile, the medication came to be prescribed for less ill people,' says Kramer. Happily, the people with severe but not intense depression appeared to be those who benefited most from the drug, and it is for this group that Prozac and other SSRIs have come to be widely used in the United States.

This Prozac phenomenon has not yet occurred in Britain, partly because of general suspicion of mood-changing medication, but also because the government has consistently dissuaded family doctors from prescribing these modern drugs on the grounds that they are 'not cost-effective'. This means that it is important, if you are considering an antidepressant, to make sure you know exactly which one is being prescribed and what the side-effects are. Most experts in postnatal depression recommend SSRIs as 'very suitable for the postnatally depressed mother on account of the lack of sedative side effects and relatively rapid antidepressant response.' It has even been suggested that SSRIs are particularly effective in the postnatal period because part of their effect is to moderate the biogenic amine's sensitivity to the hormonal changes occurring at this time. Out of the four SSRIs currently available in Britain, Seroxat is licensed for panic attacks and is thought to be the drug of choice if anxiety and panic are among the symptoms, whereas Prozac helps more when the person feels flat.

Can antidepressants be used safely during pregnancy and breastfeeding?

Women are bombarded with information about potential damage that can be done to the fetus as a result of a wide range of influences from soft cheeses to alcohol and cigarettes, and above all, drugs. Most women are rightly reluctant to consider the use of medication during pregnancy and until recently the medical consensus was that antidepressants should not be used either in pregnancy or during breastfeeding. Women who were put on antidepressants after the birth of a child were always advised to stop breastfeeding before starting the course.

Yet it now seems probable that many antidepressants can be used safely during this time. 'Fortunately for the psychiatric health of mothers,' says Dr Riley, 'few adverse effects are attributable to psychotropic drugs' (drugs that have an effect on the mind). Many women, for instance, who are schizophrenic or manic depressive are maintained on strong psychotropic drugs known as neuroleptics throughout pregnancy, with an almost complete absence of fetal abnormality resulting – even though small quantities of the drugs do get through to the baby either through the placenta or the mother's milk. The same seems to happen with antidepressants – small amounts (about 1/40th of the adult dose) enter the breast milk, but not enough to have any effect.

There is no point, however, in using antidepressants if they are going to make you feel more anxious. It's important to read as widely as you can about the subject, discuss all your concerns with your doctor or health visitor and make up your mind about what is best for you and your baby.

Hormone therapy

Until recently, the consensus among psychiatrists at least was that the best treatment for postnatal depression was with antidepressants. However, a recent study carried out jointly by psychiatrists and gynaecologists and published in *The Lancet* in

April 1996 suggests that oestrogen therapy, using patches similar to those used in hormone replacement therapy (HRT), may be effective in treating the condition. The women in the trial were selected because they became severely depressed within three months of the birth of their baby – and half of those put on patches had had no apparent benefit from six weeks of antidepressant treatment. During the first month of treatment the women on oestrogen therapy improved rapidly, including those who had not responded to antidepressants – leading doctors to suggest that oestrogen may work faster than antidepressants and be more effective for some women.

So, can depression be caused by fluctuating hormones and thus cured by hormone therapy? The jury is still out and there are conflicting reports about the role of hormones in depression. In November 1996, a large study of menopausal women, another time of life when hormone levels are known to change, found no evidence at all that the depression in women at the time of the menopause had a link with hormone changes. However, another study published in the same month found that some women suffering from ME, or Chronic Fatigue Syndrome, had significantly lowered levels of oestrogen and that their symptoms of extreme exhaustion improved dramatically both when they were pregnant – and therefore oestrogen levels increased – and also when they were given oestrogen patches as well as cyclical progesterone.

The consensus is that so far it is too early to say whether oestrogen therapy can help the symptoms of postnatal depression. More research is needed and is currently underway – so watch out for media coverage of the results. In the mean time, it may be that your doctor will suggest oestrogen patches as well as treatment with antidepressants. There is no evidence that using both therapies together carries any risks.

Psychiatric mother and baby units

Admission to hospital is rarely necessary in the treatment of postnatal depression. But in severe depression and particularly in the treatment of postnatal psychosis where infanticide or suicide is a possibility, it can be essential. Although children's wards in hospital almost always have space available for parents to stay, it is still common for mentally ill mothers to be admitted to adult psychiatric wards which have no adequate facilities for the baby to come too. This situation is changing, but only slowly.

There are, however, a few excellent mother and baby units where women can be observed and accurately diagnosed. These special units allow the mother time and space to express her emotions, thoughts, preoccupations and misinterpretations almost as they occur. She can watch other mothers with their babies and learn from them and from nurses how to care for and play with her baby. And, says psychiatrist Professor Ian Brockington, who set up a mother and baby unit in Birmingham, 'she can gradually receive the powerful reinforcement a baby provides for those who please him or her.' Admission without the baby, he says, is worse than useless as it destroys self-confidence, independence and the mother–baby relationship.

Day care is available in some large towns. At the prototype 'parent and baby day unit' in Hanley, near Stoke on Trent, eight out of every hundred mothers in the local population are referred for therapy, along with husbands, relatives and older children if considered necessary. These include women who are severely depressed as well as those with milder conditions. The unit consists of a day room, a nursery, kitchen, group room, and several offices, and there are a large number of staff including psychiatric nurses, occupational therapists, nursery nurses, a psychologist and a psychiatrist. Such models of care are gradually becoming more widely available.

CHAPTER 7

Looking after yourself

Is This All There Is?

The sound of a cry, a nappy to change,
Bottles to wash and sleep's out of range.
A little girl constantly calling for Mummy,
While baby still cries and you can't find the dummy.

The washing machine is a constant drone.
You can't find a moment to spend on your own.
There's carpets to hoover and plenty to dust.
There's no time for ironing but cooking's a must.

It's just indescribable, this whole new life.
No warning of this when he asked "Be me wife?"
No passion, no glamour, no romance or fun,
Just a babbling daughter and a crying new son.

There's no one to talk to, all day on my own.
There's not even anyone home I can phone.
Can't go for a walk, it's pouring with rain,
It feels like my whole life's been poured down the drain.

Day in and day out, week upon week.
Days are all routine and nights short of sleep.
A husband who works very hard for his pay,
And even his wage barely covers the way.

My children are sixteen months older now,
And can do a bit more than just cry and howl.
Heidi gives me a hug, Matthew kisses my cheek,
Just a small ray of sunshine to help through the week.

∽ ∽ ∽

Kay, the young mother who wrote this poem, lives in a remote village with no public transport and no car of her own. She coped well with her first child. But she realized there was something wrong within weeks of the birth of her second.

'I didn't feel any love for him. I just didn't want to know. He was a good baby when he was little but as he got older, he'd cry instead of learning to talk. I couldn't bear it. I'd cry for hours on end and getting so angry with the children. I treated them as I wouldn't want another adult to treat me. I felt as though I was stuck in a situation that I couldn't change and I had no control over.'

By the time Matthew was a year old, Kay felt as though she'd hit rock bottom. 'I was hiding it all from my husband, or trying to. I'd stop crying when he got home from work. I didn't want him to know how bad I was feeling – or anyone else. In any case, I couldn't put my feelings into words. I knew something was wrong but I couldn't put my finger on exactly what it was. And I felt it wouldn't be fair to dump all my problems on anyone. But he got pretty fed-up with me even so. I know he was thinking about leaving me at one point.

'Eventually, I left a message on the health visitor's answerphone, asking her to phone me urgently. She came to see me two days later and stayed for two hours. We talked about everything and she told me that she was fairly sure I had postnatal depression. I'd never heard of it before. It was a tremendous relief just to hear that there was a name for the way I was feeling. She talked to the doctor for me, for which I was grateful because I was embarrassed to talk about it myself. The GP put me on antidepressants and within a few weeks I felt able to carry on. I went off the Pill which I think had made my mood swings worse and gradually life has got better.

'I know that my life will really change for the better when both the children are at school and I can get back to work. That's still two years away. But I can live with that. I can see now that things won't always be as difficult as they are now, that they won't stay like this forever. I talk to my husband about the way that I feel even when I feel lousy. We've talked so much in the past few months, perhaps more than we've ever done before. And nearly every week, volunteers from an organization called Families Matter come to my house. They've become friends but they also know so much about my condition. I can ask them advice and I know that I can depend on them and trust them.

'I still can't afford a car. But I can sometimes borrow my mum's car to take the children to the playgroup a couple of times a week. And I'm on the committee of the Mother and Toddlers group which means that I get out in the evening once in a while, which is important. And I try to do things I enjoy – painting, needlework and this poetry. The other day when the kids were running riot I wrote an angry poem called 'I Need My Peace'. In the end it turned out quite funny and made me feel better.'

Kay's experience is not untypical. When she finally looked for help, the support was there for her. Her health visitor knew straight away what was wrong with her. Her GP was able to provide the right medication. And even though she was geographically isolated, she gets weekly support from people who are able to help her.

The tragedy is that it took so long for Kay to reach out for help. Thousands of women are like Kay – they know that things aren't right but are unable or unwilling to ask for help. It is vital that friends or relatives of women in Kay's situation put aside any judgemental feelings they may have and help them to get the support that is ready and waiting.

Postnatal depression can never be entirely prevented, but there are ways in which parents can help themselves to better emotional health. Here are 20 golden rules to help your self to stay healthy when you have a baby.

1. Arrange to talk through the birth afterwards

You may feel a need to talk through your experience of giving birth, not just to friends but to the professionals who attended you. This is especially likely if the labour was difficult or traumatic or resulted in an emergency Caesarean. It is your right to have that wish respected and it is now considered good obstetric practice for midwives to make themselves available after the birth so that you can ask any questions that are on your mind, or perhaps express your concern about the way aspects of the birth were handled. You can only benefit from being as honest as possible – what's more midwives can learn from your honesty. It may even be worthwhile finding the time to write a full account of any traumatic events to help you make sense of the experience.

2. Don't forget that you are entitled to support if your baby is ill

If your baby is born premature and admitted to hospital, or is ill or disabled, you and your partner are in need of sensitive and gentle support and you should expect to receive it.

3. Remember that breastfeeding isn't a moral imperative

'The best things that could happen to women today is for wet-nursing to be brought back,' says one leading health visitor. And from her position of having seen hundreds of women demoralized by their 'failure' to breastfeed properly, she's only half joking. Breastfeeding is good for your baby and a good way for you both to get to know each other. If you have problems, remember that this may be a symptom of your depression. Instead of giving up straight away, try coasting for a while, perhaps supplementing breast with bottle. However, if you are unable to breastfeed, it's important to remember that millions of healthy, happy people were bottlefed without suffering any disadvantage.

4. Don't feel that you have to play host to visitors

You're likely to get extra visitors in the weeks after the baby's born. Every new parent wants to show off their baby but you don't have to play hostess. Tell friends and relatives to stop off at the delicatessen on the way to the house. And remember they're coming to see you and the baby, not to check up on how clean the house is. Don't worry about mess and dirt – and if anyone else worries, let them give the house a quick spring clean while they're visiting!

5. Take it a day at a time

Don't expect to become a skilled parent overnight. And don't assume that from day one you're going to feel good about this huge commitment that you've taken on. If you don't feel good at first, it doesn't mean that you'll never feel good again. Remember you've just completed a major nine-month plan which ended with a physically intensive trial of labour. Straightaway, while your mental and physical reserves are at their lowest, you're faced with an infinitely bigger challenge. Take it slowly. Think about the day and how you're going to cope with it and above all, how you're going to take good care of yourself during that day.

6. Don't blame yourself when things go wrong

You're bound to have adverse as well as pleasurable reactions to becoming a mother. What turns transitory exhaustion, bewilderment and anxiety into depression is guilt and shame. 'If you are ashamed of your anger, ashamed of your lethargy, ashamed of

133

not being able to cope then the guilt strikes very deep, especially at a time when these feelings seem so inappropriate,' says Robert Holden, the man who proved in a 1996 BBC TV *QED* programme that you can learn to be happy. 'Here's everybody celebrating the new baby. And you are feeling like the pits. In our society, depression is always shameful. We have organizations like Depressives Anonymous because no one can bear to admit that they are depressed. For new mothers, that combination of guilt and fear of the future can be unbearable.'

7. Talk about your feelings honestly to at least one other person

Bottling up emotions and feelings leads to depression. Make sure that you have at least one person to whom you can talk freely without fear of criticism or ridicule. It may be that you already have a partner, friend or family member who you know will understand. It's more likely that you are out of practice at talking in this way. You may have to explain to someone close to you why it's important that they listen to you. And if that doesn't work, you may have to go further afield. The important thing is that acknowledging your feelings out loud is the first step to distancing yourself from them. Remember that the feelings are not you. You are not the depression. You are suffering from depression. It's a vital distinction.

8. Learn to speak your mind – especially to your partner

Even if you decide not to take your partner as your main confidant, it's still important to be 'up front' in your interaction with him. Most advice to new parents is to avoid 'time-wasting' rows, to hold your tongue on irritable remarks and, if necessary, to tell your partner that you're not interested in criticism at the moment. This is not necessarily good advice. By becoming parents, your lives have changed irreversibly – most of all with the first child but substantially with subsequent children. You have to draw apart to make space for the new baby and that means the two of you moving as individuals in different directions. You can try to pretend that nothing serious has happened but the chances are you'll end up screaming at each other.

The healthy way forward is to try to voice all your feelings, however difficult they are – and let your partner have his say too. Make talking a priority. You don't have to persuade your partner to agree with you – or agree with what he has to say. That's not the point. You will inevitably have different views on child rearing because you were both brought up in different ways, perhaps in different traditions and cultures. But you will feel more confident and less resentful if you feel that your emotions have been given an airing and treated with respect. And your partner will feel the same way too.

9. Find ways to be kind to yourself

Make yourself a priority, even if that means making sacrifices in other parts of your life. As Dr Holden says:

Being a martyr won't make you a better mother. When a mother neglects herself, she's also neglecting her baby. Children, in the first few years especially, are like loudspeakers coming off your own experience. If you feel lousy, they'll feel lousy. If you feel good, they'll feel good. It's almost a mathematical equation. invest this much time in yourself and you'll see your child smile. Invest some more time in yourself and watch your child laughing. Martyrdom is giving out the wrong signals. If you don't put yourself joint first, then you are teaching your child that life is about sacrifice. It's giving them an agenda for misery. That's poor teaching.

10. Let your mother take the strain

Remember the benefits experienced by Japanese women who traditionally spend the first month or two in their mother's home. If you have a good relationship with your mother, get her to come and stay with you – not just for a day or two but for as long as she can. And if there's going to be disruption at your home, if you're moving house, for instance, or having the house decorated or an extension built or you haven't got room for her to stay with you, then go and stay with her. Don't look at it as a cop-out but as an investment in the future.

If you don't get on with your mother or if she lives too far away or is dead, then try and find another older woman whom you can see regularly and talk over problems as they arise. That may be a neighbour, a friend or relative or a health visitor. And if you can afford it, pay someone to do the washing and cleaning at least for a few weeks. It may be worth putting aside some money specifically for that purpose.

11. Get plenty of sleep

The need for regular, refreshing sleep does not disappear when you become a mother. Every hour of sleep we miss, we need to catch up on or it catches up on us. Studies show that, on average, women sleep for seven and a half hours a night. For mothers of newborn babies, this is reduced to six and a quarter hours – not a dramatic loss overall but there is a big reduction in deep sleep and an increase in very light sleep. This inevitably cause an increase in irritability and a tendency for mood swings.

Accept offers of help looking after the baby while you sleep – or ask for it. Cancel visitors if it means you having to miss out on a possible nap. If your partner is out at work all day, explain that you need to sleep when he gets home and is able to look after the baby. It's important to spend time with your partner, but when you're tired after the birth, sleep comes first. If necessary, spend a night or two away from the baby – you can express milk for night feeds if breastfeeding – so that you can catch up.

Bathing and massage can also help you to sleep better and more deeply. Before the birth, stock up with some of the essential oils that will help you recover afterwards – or ask friends to buy them for you as presents (some essential oils, such as ylang ylang, are expensive but worth it). In her book, *Aromatherapy for*

Mother and Baby, aromatherapist Allison England recommends the following oils for postnatal bathing:

- Lavender oil helps to heal the perineum. Take a bottle into hospital with you and sprinkle a few drops in a warm bath.

- Ylang ylang, bergamot, jasmine, neroli and clary sage will help to lift the spirits. Sprinkle two or three drops of oil in the bath or put a few drops on a tissue to sniff if you are suffering from the baby blues.

- Lavender, marjoram and Roman camomile will help you sleep. Put three drops of oil in a warm bath just before you go to bed. And sprinkle a few drops of lavender oil on your pillow to make sleep more pleasant – you can top it up after a night-time feed.

- Two or three drops of either geranium or bergamot oil with two or three drops of rosemary oil in a warm bath in the morning will help to set you up for the day.

Having your back and shoulders massaged at the end of a long day can help you relax and sleep well. If you're breastfeeding, keep the massage oil very weak. It's safe to add one or two drops of essential oil to every teaspoon of carrier oil (available from an aromatherapist). Add three drops of lavender, three drops of rosemary and three drops of geranium oil to one and a half to two teaspoons of carrier oil.

Massaging your baby is not only therapeutic for both you and the baby, it's also wonderfully enjoyable, relaxes both of you and promotes sleep. Allison England recommends the following: Put five tablespoons of slightly warmed (placed in a bowl of warm water) almond, coconut or jojoba oil and add two or three drops of Roman camomile, rose, neroli or lavender oil.

She says the best time to give the massage is after your baby has been bathed or in between nappy changes – but not when tired, hungry or fretful. Make sure the room is warm, that your nails are short and that any scratchy jewellery is removed. Sit on the floor with your legs outstretched, a large towel placed over your lap and the baby on top, or put the baby in the middle of a large bed. Lie the baby on his back and using both hands, start from the ankles and massage a small amount of oil up to the tops of the legs and then glide your hands down again to the feet – repeat three or four times. Massage the soles of the feet with your thumb in both directions three or four times – this is very calming for the baby. Massage the stomach in a clockwise direction and then move up to the shoulders and glide gently down the arms to the wrists and up to the shoulders again, repeating the action three or four times. If the baby is still happy, turn him over and massage the back of the legs from ankles to bottom. Place your hands on the top of the buttocks and glide them with one hand on either side of the spine up to the neck and out over the shoulders and back down the sides of the body to the buttocks again. Avoid the hands as you don't want the oil going in his mouth.

12. Make sure that you eat well

Your energy and immune system are depleted after childbirth and breastfeeding can take away your strength even further. So it's extra important to eat good food. Each day, you should aim to eat:

- 6 to 11 servings of bread, cereal, rice or pasta

- 3 to 5 servings of vegetables

- 2 to 4 servings of fruit

- 2 to 3 servings of milk, yoghurt or cheese

- 2 to 3 servings of meat, poultry, fish or eggs

- Sparing amounts of fat, oils and sweets.

When you are depressed, it's normal to crave 'comfort' foods, such as chocolate, biscuits and cakes. However, these fatty, sugar-rich foods will not make you feel better in the long run as your weight goes up and your self-esteem sinks. Try to find the nonfatty foods that will fulfil this role for you. It has been suggested that certain foods raise the serotonin levels in the brain and thus make you feel better. Foods in this category include dates, bread, bananas, hazelnuts, cauliflower, potatoes, raw onions, garlic and lettuce, camomile and peppermint tea.

To combat physical exhaustion after childbirth, Dr Keith Souter makes the following recommendations in his book *Get Well Soon*:

Do:

- Take proteins from white meat, fish, free-range eggs, lentils, soya, yoghurt and cheese. Oily fish such as salmon, trout, mackerel, sardines and herring three times a week will give you an extra boost.

- Eat wholemeal bread, plenty of bran-based cereals, potatoes, beans and vegetables.

- Use raw vegetables in salads as much as possible. Cooking them destroys vitamins and causes the leaching out of many vitamins.

- Ensure a daily intake of antioxidant-containing vegetables – all red or orange vegetables.

- Eat a least two pieces of fruit every day.

- Eat a handful of dried fruit three times a week.

- Eat a handful of nuts (walnuts, unsalted peanuts or almonds) three times a week.

- Use olive oil, sunflower or corn oil for cooking, adding to salads or for soaking baked potatoes in.

- Drink fresh milk and fresh fruit juice, preferably home-made, every day.

- Eat spinach, sea-food and garlic regularly. These foods are thought to help lift depression.

- Eat plenty of honey – it's thought to protect against anxiety.

Don't:

- Start smoking again, especially if you gave up while you were pregnant.

- Drink too much alcohol.

- Eat too much red meat – alternate with white meat and fish.

- Eat refined or processed foods.

- Eat chocolate or sweets.

- Buy soft, fizzy drinks.

- Eat tinned, smoked or pickled foods.

- Add too much salt or sugar to foods or drinks.

After the birth you are likely to have reduced levels of vitamins B and C, calcium, iron, magnesium, potassium and zinc. Many of these deficiencies can be boosted simply by having a bowl of fortified cereal every morning – Cornflakes will do splendidly. Or you may prefer to take a good multivitamin supplement or food supplement.

13. Remember that exercise beats depression

As well as helping you get your figure back, exercise improves your physical and mental health, induces a feeling of well-being, relaxation and being in control of your body. It also makes you feel you are giving time for yourself. You won't feel like taking up regular exercise immediately after having a baby, although you will need to start your pelvic floor exercises as soon as possible, of course. Walking every day with the baby in the pram is worth while as soon as you have got the energy, and however unlikely it may seem at first, it's worth making an effort to get to an exercise class as soon as you possibly can. You are far more likely to keep it up if you go to a class rather than exercise by yourself at home, however enticing the video seems.

Research shows that at least half of women with postnatal

depression are cured by regular exercise. Which exercise doesn't really matter. The important thing is that you enjoy it enough to do it fairly regularly.

∽ ∽ ∽

'There's something about the routine of a class that's tremendously therapeutic,' says Toni who returned to her weekly jazz dance class within a couple of months of the birth of each of her three children, choosing a class which meant her husband could baby-sit their growing brood. 'It's really good to see the same people every week even if you're not particularly good friends with them and just say "hi, how's it going?". Obviously it's good for your health. But what you don't realize is how good it is for your soul – at least not until you stop going for a while and realize how little things are niggling at you and how tense you've become. I know so many women who've hung on to a regular class when they've been low and life's been hard and they've realized later that it was that hour every week that made the rest of it bearable.'

∽ ∽ ∽

It may be a good idea to avoid over-energetic aerobic or step classes – in fact, their health benefits are disputed by many experts. Instead try and find a class which specializes in dance, stretch, t'ai chi, yoga or water aerobics which are gentler on the anatomy. Some health authorities have set up 'exercise on prescription' programmes, through which you can be referred to a local leisure centre staffed by trained physiotherapists by your GP. You will be assessed by a doctor and then prescribed exercise tailor-made for your condition and because people go regularly, there's an opportunity to socialize.

If you are stuck at home, you could try something like shiatsu, a method of Japanese stretching and pressure point work that's been practised as a form of family healing for thousands of years. Here are a few shiatsu exercises designed to beat stress which you may be able to work into your daily routine.

- In the morning, practise deep breathing. Breathe in on a count of five and out on a count of five and repeat six times. This is a way of expanding your inner space.

- If you feel stressed – lock your fingers together, invert your hands and stretch your arms up to the ceiling. Breathe in, hold for a count of five and then breathe out as you lower your arms. Hunch up your shoulders as you breathe in and then breathe out as you let them drop. Repeat six times.

- Make your fingers into a fork and place them one inch behind each ear, lift your elbows and squeeze your fingers down the back of your neck.

- For shoulder pains and backache, use your hand to pinch the loose flesh on the top of your shoulders. Hold it for a few seconds and then let go.

14. Be prepared to make a new circle of friends

This can be one of the most difficult things for new mothers, especially first-time mothers. Women who have been in full-time work or who have moved house – a common event close to childbirth – will be in need of new friendships. It's possible that you may have a baby at the same time as an existing friend but more than likely you'll need to travel to see them. What you need is a circle of friends with babies round about the same age who live near enough to drop in for cups of tea and go for walks in the park together. It's been shown repeatedly that regular, close contact with women sharing similar problems, concerns and needs is the best way to beat postnatal depression. But it's often very difficult to know how to get started.

For many new mothers it will seem too much effort to start the process of making friends from scratch. You may feel that you will have little in common with other mothers – apart from your baby and why should that be a basis for friendship? You may even feel that you are more intelligent, better dressed or just better than the women you see pushing prams. 'I used to go past a playground on the way to work when I was pregnant and seeing groups of frumpy women sitting together gossiping and thinking, surely I'm not going to end up like that,' recalls Janice. 'But by the next summer, there I was, though it was a different playground. A few of us used to meet up most days either in the park or at someone's house and we'd have a wicked time.'

It may be difficult to find the right place to meet other mothers, especially if you're the only mother in your street who is staying at home. Don't automatically assume that organized methods of meeting new people are not for you. The National Childbirth Trust is a useful source of socializing. If you joined an NCT class when you were pregnant, the chances are the mothers in the class will continue to meet for coffee mornings afterwards. If you didn't, contact the NCT (see Useful addresses) and ask them about local contacts. Your health visitor will also be a good source of information on local facilities.

Other organizations include the following:

- *Meet-a-Mum* is a voluntary scheme where groups of mothers – and sometimes fathers – meet regularly, sometimes several times a week, in each other's homes. A new mother is given the name of the local organizer who will provide information about where local meetings are due to take place. 'We don't just exist for women with clinical depression. It can be very lonely being a new mother and it makes a big difference to meet up with people in the same situation,' says local organizer Bev Billyer. 'It can take a lot of guts to turn up at someone's house and meet a group of people who all know each other. I was terrified when I first went. And we get some people who come once and don't come again. But it made all the difference to my life. We meet socially for a good time as well as the meetings where people can talk about their problems.'

- *Newpin* operates from comfortable, home-like premises with a living room, playroom and kitchen where 'isolated women can make friends and gain support in an emotionally secure environment'. A woman is allocated a 'friend' and can join a training group to become one who befriends others. Training includes sessions with a counsellor who helps the woman explore her own feelings. Women are referred by health visitors, social workers or GPs or you can refer yourself. The only criteria for inclusion is that you are a mother or the main carer of children. Studies show that one third of women with depression who attend recover completely and almost all become less depressed. It improves the relationship with the partner and the couple's children.

- *Homestart* is a voluntary home visiting programme with over 100 branches operating all over the UK. The volunteers are 'realistically recruited, carefully prepared, sensitively matched with only one or two families and meticulously supported' by the organizers who eventually train the visitees to become visitors.

Local contacts for all these organizations can be found by telephoning the national headquarters listed under Useful addresses at the end of the book.

15. Remember that a small change can make all the difference

Try to identify small changes to your life that will make a big difference. Passing your driving test, for example, could improve the quality of your life.

16. Take control of the day

It's easy to feel as though you can't get anything done when you have a baby to look after. Most new mothers feel like this because just adjusting to the baby is a huge task and it's important to remember that the feeling won't last for ever. Psychologists Ann Dunnewold and Diane Sanford recommend the following plan to help you cope better. First, single out one area in which you do have control – even if it's just getting the baby's nappy changed when it's needed. You *are* succeeding here. Write down on a piece of paper: 'I am getting the baby's nappies changed every day' and pin it on the wall or on your kitchen notice board.

Then decide on one task that you will get done – making the bed, cleaning one room or always keeping one room clean. Slowly add one more task at a time, never adding more than you can expect to accomplish. Talk to a friend or your partner about ways of getting the basic chores done. You may be able to afford to hire someone to help clean your house. Or perhaps a friend will do your shopping until you've got more energy. Get take-away food a few times a week. The main thing is to focus your mind on what you're accomplishing instead of just seeing every-thing that's still not done.

17. Make sure you get rid of anger

Unfortunately, there are too often reasons for anger when you have a baby. You may feel annoyed that your partner, parent, friend is not more supportive. You may feel that you should be getting more sleep and be feeling better sooner. If you push anger down inside you, it may explode over something minor which can leave you feeling uncomfortably out of control. Ann Dunnewold and Diane Sanford have the following excellent proposals for working out angry feelings:

> Punch a pillow, throw or kick a ball, break eggs in the sink, blow up a paper bag and pop it. Take a shower and scream or scream in your car with all the windows rolled up. Or scream silently: clench your fists, tense your shoulders, prepare to scream but let only the air, not the noise out of your mouth. Write out your feel-ings in a journal or scribble them on paper. Tear paper or phone books. Make ugly, angry faces in the mirror. Go out into the back garden and stomp around. Make a list of your favourite anger activities and pin it on the noticeboard in case you forget them because you're so cross.
>
> If you're going to accuse someone else, try to be assertive rather than aggressive. Use the word 'I' rather than 'you'. And stick to the event at hand rather than the last 40 anger-provoking events in your life – and be specific about what's been done and

*what you'd like to have done differently. For example, say: 'I was
angry when you walked in and right past me to the baby. I'd like
you to greet me first.' This may get you a solution much quicker
than saying: 'You are so heartless – you ignore me all the time.'*

18. Learn how to deal with panic

Here's a 10-point plan to beat panic symptoms:

1. Remember that the feelings are no more than an exagger-
    ation of the normal bodily reactions to stress.

2. They are not in the least harmful or dangerous – just unpleas-
    ant. Nothing worse will happen.

3. Stop adding to panic with frightening thoughts about what
    is happening and where it might lead.

4. Describe to yourself what is really happening in your body
    at this moment, not what you fear might happen.

5. Now wait and give the fear time to pass without fighting it
    or running away from it. Just accept it.

6. Notice that once you stop adding to it with frightening
    thoughts, the fear starts to fade away by itself.

7. Remember that the whole point of practice is learning how to
    cope with fear without avoiding it so this is an opportunity
    to make progress.

8. Think about the progress you have made so far despite all
    the difficulties and how pleased you will be when you
    succeed this time.

9. Now begin to describe your surroundings to yourself and
    plan out in your mind exactly what to do next.

10. Then when you are ready to go, start off in an easy, relaxed
    way. There is no need for effort or hurry.

19. Don't try to be the perfect mother – it takes up too much energy

When you have a baby, it's worth while making an effort to accept that you are not going to be able to control your life in the way you used to. You can't always make the baby sleep or stop crying. Your house may be a mess and you may not look the way you'd like to. You have to make sure of some things – paying the bills, changing the baby's nappy and making sure there's enough food in the house – but you don't have to be strict in other areas. It's worth making a conscious decision to let go and no longer be the person in charge of everything and everyone.

Remind yourself that all you have to be is a good-enough parent and a good-enough partner, a good-enough friend and a good-enough daughter. You don't actually get extra points for being better than good-enough. And you'll also have the space, the time and the mental balance to enjoy your life, enjoy your relationships and enjoy your growing child.

20. Let go of the reins

When alcoholics give up drink with AA, they learn that the only way they'll succeed is to accept that they are powerless over their lives and to hand over control to a 'higher power'. 'Let go and let God' is one of their popular slogans (with God representing a fairly nebulous outside force). There are not many ways in which having a baby is like recovering from alcohol addiction, but there could be a connection here. A new parent will inevitably find that they come up against the experience of being powerless to control their tiny offspring. 'I kept asking myself who's this little guy turning everybody's life upside down?', as one mother put it. It's important to recognize and acknowledge this feeling and to accept that you are not in control. Psychologists call this 'learned helplessness' and recommend it as an emotional energy-saving mechanism. It may seem like weakness, but admitting, on a daily basis, that you're powerless over your new baby, your topsy-turvy emotions, your relationship with those close to you, your new life with the extra family member, might just be the key to discovering the strength and energy you need for the little guy.

There isn't a simple way to make the early months of parenthood free of stress or depression. For all sorts of reasons, men and women today have to make a whole series of sometimes painful adjustments at the start of family life. This book may seem to have made depressing reading at times but its intention is to reassure those struggling to find a way forward that there is light at the end of the tunnel. Many of the ideas from doctors, psychotherapists, health visitors and other professionals that you've read about may seem unfamiliar and different from the traditional way of looking at parenting. You probably won't agree with all of them, but thinking about them and talking them through with friends, relatives, other parents and health visitors should make the baby blues easier to survive.

Bibliography

Brockington, Ian: *Motherhood and Mental Health*. Oxford
   University Press, 1996
Clement, Dr Sarah: *The Caesarean Experience*. HarperCollins,
   1991
Cox, John and Holden, Jeni: *Perinatal Psychiatry*. Gaskell, 1994
Dalton, Katharina: *Depression After Childbirth*. Oxford
   Paperbacks, third edition, 1996
Daws, Dilys: *Through the Night: Helping Parents and Sleepless
   Infants*. Free Association Books, 1993
Dunnewold, Ann and Sanford, Diane G.: *Postpartum Survival
   Guide*. New Harbinger Publications, 1994
England, Allison: *Aromatherapy for Mother and Baby*. Vermilion,
   1993
Ferguson, Pamela: *The Self-Shiatsu Handbook*. Newleaf, 1995
Holden, Robert: *Stressbusters*. Thorsons, 1992
Kramer, Peter D.: *Listening to Prozac*. Viking, 1993
McConville, Brigid: *Beating the Blues*. Headline, 1996
Parr, Mel A.: *Support for Couples in the Transition to Parenthood*
   (PhD thesis, 1996, available £20 from M. Parr, tel: 01438
   748478)
Raphael-Leff, Joan: *Pregnancy: The Inside Story*. Insight
   Professional, 1993
Raphael-Leff, Joan: *Psychological Processes of Childbearing*.
   Chapman & Hall, 1991
Riley, Diana: *Perinatal Mental Health: A Sourcebook for Health
   Professionals*. Radcliffe Medical Press, 1995

Rowe, Dorothy: *Depression: The Way Out of Your Prison.*
Routledge, second edition, 1996

Smith, Gerrilyn and Nairne, Kathy: *Dealing with Depression.* The
Women's Press, 1996

Souter, Dr Keith: *Get Well Soon.* CW Daniel Co., 1996

Stern, Malcolm: *Courage to Love.* Piatkus, 1996

Wildwood, Christine: *Aromatherapy, Massage with Essential Oils.*
Health Essentials, 1991

Wurtzel, Elizabeth: *Prozac Nation: Young and Depressed in America.*
Quartet Books, 1995

Useful addresses

AIMS (Association for Improvements in the Maternity Services, providing support to arrange the kind of birth you want and making a complaint)
40 Kingswood Avenue, London NW6 6SL.
tel: 0181 960 5585

Association for Infant Mental Health UK
Tavistock Centre, 120 Belsize Lane, London NW3 5BA

Association for Postnatal Illness (APNI)
25 Jerdan Place, London SW6 1BE.
tel: 0171 386 0868

British Association for Counselling
1 Regent Place, Rugby CV21 2PJ.
tel: 01788 550899

British Association of Psychotherapists
37 Mapesbury Road, London NW2 4HJ.
tel: 0181 452 9823

Crysis (support group for parents whose children cry excessively)
BM Crysis, London WC1N 3XX.
tel: 0171 404 5011

Homestart
2 Salisbury Rd, Leicester LE1 7QR.
tel: 01533 554988

Issue (National Fertility Association)
509 Aldridge Rd, Great Barr, Birmingham B44 8NA.
tel: 0121 344 4414

La Leche League (for breastfeeding advice)
BM 3424, London WC1X 6XX.
tel: 0171 242 1278

Meet-a-Mum Association (MAMA)
58 Malden Avenue, South Norwood, London SE25 4HS.
tel: 0181 656 7318

National Childbirth Trust
Alexandra House, Oldham Terrace, London W3 6NH.
tel: 0181 992 8637

Newpin (support network and drop-in centre for vulnerable
families with children)
35 Sutherland Square, Walworth, London SE17 3EE.
tel: 0171 703 6326

Parentline
(confidential helpline) 01702 559900

PIPPIN (Parent–Infant Programme)
'Derwood', Todds Green, Stevenage SG1 2JE.
tel: 01438 748478

North America

Depression after Delivery
PO Box 1282, Morrisville, PA 19067, USA.
tel: (215) 295-3994; (800)944-4PPD

Postpartum Support International,
   927 N. Kellogg Avenue, Santa Barbara, CA 93111, USA.
   tel: (805)967-7636
Postpartum Adjustment Support Services (PASS-CAN)
   PO Box 7282, Oakville, Ontario, Canada
   L6J 6C6.
   tel: (905) 844-9009

Australia

International Childbirth Education Association
   14 Clemisdon Avenue, Roseville, NSW 2069

Parents' Centres Australia
   45 Albion Street, Harris Park, NSW 2150

New Zealand

International Childbirth Education Association
   102 Cannington Road, Dunedin, Otago 9001

Federation of New Zealand Parent Centres Incorporated
   PO Box 17-351, Wellington

Index

abortion as a cause of postnatal
    depression 60, 120
Abrams, Rebecca 111
abuse 59, 92, 120
adoption 44, 52
advice, unhelpful 97–8
aerobics 141
age of mother 56–7
alcohol 140
alcoholism 147
Anderson, Pamela 46
anger 32, 145–6
antenatal care 72–3, 79–81
antenatal classes 28, 55, 58, 94
antidepressants 76, 116, 122–5
    and breastfeeding 126
anxiety 32–3
appetite, loss of 35–6
aromatherapy 136–8
Asian women 48, 49
assertiveness 145–6
Association for Postnatal Illness
    12, 151
attention deficit disorder 101

babies
    ability to detect fraudulence
        106
    bonding with 62, 63

born with an abnormality
    63, 132
colic 62
'conversations' with mother
    99–101
crying at night 62
effect of postnatal depression
    on 101–2
emotionally mismatched with
    mother 64
massage 137–8
night-time feeds 85
relationship with 62–4
weaning 53
baby blues 24–6
backache 142
baths 136
Beale, Caroline 23
Billyer, Bev 143
biogenic amines 124, 125
biological factors 52–4
birth
    difficulties 49–50
    men's role 88
    new model of care during 81–2
    obstetric care 73–4
    professional care after 82–3
    talking about afterwards 132
bonding 12, 25, 31–2, 62–4, 112

breastfeeding 103
  antidepressants and 76, 126
  aromatherapy and 137
  expressing milk 136
  father's jealousy of 109
  hormones 53
  night-time feeds 85
  problems 132–3
  weaning 53
breathing exercises 142
British Association of
  Psychotherapists 122
British Medical Association 97
Broadbent, Anne 39–40
Brockington, Ian 15, 62, 128

Caesarean section 49, 132
career mothers 98
childcare 98, 99–100, 112
childhood experiences 59, 66–7, 92
Chronic Fatigue Syndrome 127
Clement, Dr Sarah 49–50, 78
clinics, antenatal 72–3, 80–1
cognitive therapy 118–19
colic 62–3
'comfort' foods, craving for 138
communication
  talking about your feelings 134,
  135
  with your partner 94, 95,
  134–5
community psychiatric nurses
  78, 118
concentration, lack of 36
continuity of care 78
control
  keeping 58–9
  loss of 34–5
  taking control of the day 144–5
counselling 76, 77, 116, 118
Cox, John 82

Craddock, Esther 49
'craziness, normal' 26–30
crying
  baby's 62
  in postnatal depression 30–1
cultural pressures 48–9

Dalton, Dr Katharina 43–5, 53
Daws, Dilys 67, 73, 79, 102–4,
  112–13, 116, 117
day care 128
depression
  during pregnancy 19–22
  'inherited' depression 59–60, 61
  manic depression 40, 126
  in men 44, 65, 91–3
  prenatal 23–4
  see also postnatal depression
Depressives Anonymous 134
Diana, Princess of Wales 12, 43,
  70, 114
diet 138–40
difficult births 49–50
divorce 87–8
doctors 71–2, 74, 75–6, 116
Drabble, Margaret 60
drugs, antidepressants 76, 116,
  122–6
Dunnewold, Ann 27, 28, 51, 55,
  64–5, 89, 115, 144–6
dysfunctional families 92

eating 138–40
Edinburgh Postnatal Depression
  Scale 77
emotions see feelings
employment 46, 68, 86, 98, 99,
  102–4, 111, 112
endorphins 53
England, Allison 137
episiotomy 49

essential oils 136–7
exercise 140–2
exhaustion 34–5

Facilitator mothers 106–7, 109
fathering, models of 105–6, 108–9
fear, coping with 146
feelings
    after birth 25–6, 133–4
    men's 91–2
    in pregnancy 21–2
    talking about 116, 134, 135
financial problems 47–8, 86–7
first-time mothers 54–6
food 138–40
    loss of interest in 35–6
forceps delivery 49
formal guidelines, health care 78
Freud, Anna 59–60
friends
    making new friendships 142–4
    relationships with 67–9
fruit 138, 139

gender roles 87, 88
genetics 59–60
George, Malcolm 91
Goldberg, Malcolm 75
Golfar, Fiona 29
good-enough mothering 99, 112, 147
GPs 71–2, 74, 75–6
Greer, Germaine 67
grey woman syndrome 36–8
grief 60
Guatemala, research in obstetric care 73–4
guidelines, health care 78
guilt 31, 133–4

Harayan, Dr Naran 78
health professionals 71–82
health visitors
    getting help from 130, 131
    past problems in identifying postnatal depression 75
    pioneering role 13, 77–83
    talking to 59, 117–18
help 114–28
Holden, Jeni 82
Holden, Robert 134, 135
Homestart 144
hormones
    after birth 53
    during pregnancy 11, 43–4, 52–3
    hormone therapy 116, 126–7
    infertility treatment 50
    thyroid imbalance 53–4
hospitals
    antenatal clinics 72–3, 80–1
    impersonal style 71
    length of stay in 46
    obstetric care 73–4
    psychiatric mother and baby units 127–8
housework 34–5, 58, 85–6, 133, 136, 145
housing problems 47–8
hyperactive children 101
hypothyroidism 54

immune system 138
inability to cope 35
inadequacy, feelings of 31
infertility 50–1, 52
'inherited' depression 59–60, 61
irritability 34

Japan, incidence of postnatal depression 47, 135

jealousy, men 85

Kitzinger, Sheila 27
Kramer, Peter 125

labour *see* birth
The Lancet 126–7
leaflets, antenatal clinics 80
'learned helplessness' 47, 94,
        147–8
life events 18
London University, Men's Studies
        Research Group 89–90
loneliness 70
loss of interest 31
losses, unresolved 60

McKenna, Kate 88
Madonna 46
manic depression 40, 126
martyrdom 135
massage 136, 137–8
maternity leave 68, 86, 103, 111
ME 127
Meet-a-Mum 89, 143
men 84–96
    danger areas 84–7
    postnatal depression 44, 65,
        91–3
    relationship with 27–8, 64–5,
        84–7, 89–91
    role in reproduction 88–9
    support for 93–4
    talking to 134–5
    understanding each other's
        needs 89–91
menopause 127
mental health 99
midwives 72, 73, 74–5, 82, 132
minerals 140
miscarriage 60

models of mothering and
        fathering 105–12
money as focus of resentment
        86–7
MORI polls 123
mothers
    getting help from your mother
        135–6
    models of mothering 105–12
    relationship with your mother
        65–67
    role of health visitor as
        substitute mother 117
multivitamin supplements 140
Murray, Jeni 25

National Childbirth Trust 71, 143
National Health Service (NHS)
        46, 121–2
neuroleptic drugs 126
'New Man' 91
Newpin 143–4
night-time feeds 85
'normal craziness' 26–30
nurses, community psychiatric
        78, 118
nutrition 138–40

obstetric care 73–4
obstetric problems 49–52
obstetricians 74
Odent, Michel 73
oestrogen 52–3, 127
oils, essential 136–7
older mothers 56–7
organizations 143–4

pain, during labour 81–2
panic attacks 146
parental orientation 106–11
Parr, Mel 27, 42, 93–4, 95, 99, 100

Participator fathers 108
partners *see* men
pelvic floor exercises 140
perfectionists 58, 147
physiotherapists 141
PIPPIN 95
post-traumatic stress 50
postnatal care 74–6
postnatal depression
    causes 11–12
    difficulty in asking for help for
        75–6
    effect on baby 101–2
    fear of being stigmatized by 15,
        75
    getting help for 114–28
    incidence 12
    looking after yourself 129–48
    outside help 114–28
    risk factors 45–70
    symptoms 30–6
postnatal psychosis 16–17, 38–41,
    53, 127–8
potassium 140
pre-menstrual syndrome (PMS)
    44, 53
pregnancy
    depression starting in 19–22
    hormones 11, 43–4, 52–3
    unplanned or unwanted
        61–2
premature babies 63, 132
prenatal depression 23–4
'problem-focused therapy'
    118
professionals
    deficiencies in care 71–6
    improvements in the delivery
        of care 76–8
    guidelines for postnatal
        depression 79–83

progesterone 11, 44, 52–3, 127
prolactin 53
Prozac 122, 124, 125
psychiatric mother and baby units
    127–8
psychiatrists 75, 118
psychological factors 54–62
psychologists 118
psychosis, postnatal 16–17,
    38–41, 53, 127–8
psychotherapy 119–22
puerperal psychosis *see* postnatal
    psychosis

'quality time' 103

Raphael-Leff, Joan 27, 65, 69, 72,
    97, 98, 105–106, 110–11,
    119–21
Reciprocator mothers 107–8,
    110–11
Regulator mothers 107, 109–10
relationships 62–70
    with baby 62–4
    with your friends 67–9
    with your mother 65–7
    with your partner 27–8, 64–5,
        84–7, 89–91
religous pressures 48–9
Renouncer fathers 108–9, 110
research into delivery of care for
    postnatal depression 76–9
Riley, Dr Diana 21, 47, 75, 77, 126
risk factors 45–70
Rowe, Dorothy 17–18, 34, 66–7,
    68, 105
Royal College of General
    Practitioners 72
Royal College of Psychiatrists
    72, 123

Sanford, Diane 27, 28, 51, 55, 64–5, 89, 115, 144–6
schizophrenia 40, 126
Seroxat 125
sex, loss of interest in 36, 85, 94–5, 96
shiatsu 141–2
shopping 145
shoulder pains 142
sick babies 132
single parents 69, 88
sleep 136–7
  disturbances 35, 62, 85
Smith, Gerrilyn 37
smoking 140
social factors 45–9
Souter, Dr Keith 139
Spreadborough, Carmel 89, 90
SSRIs (selective serotonin reuptake inhibitors) 123, 124–5
Stern, Malcolm 84
stillbirth 60
stress, post-traumatic 50
suicide 128
support
  choosing the right 116
  difficulty in seeking 114
  talking therapy or drugs? 116–127
  when to seek outside 115
symptoms
  postnatal depression 30–6

postnatal psychosis 41

talking therapies 116–22
tearfulness 30–1
Thatcher, Margaret 113
thyroid imbalance 53–4
tranquillizers 122
tricyclic antidepressants 124, 125

unplanned pregnancies 61–2
unresolved losses 60
unwanted pregnancies 61–2

violence
  caused by depression 92
  symptom of postnatal depression 34
  cycle of 120
visitors 133, 136
vitamins 139, 140

walking 140
weaning 53
Winnicott, Donald 99
Wood, Victoria 15
work
  mothers and 46, 98–9
  different attitudes to 106 –11
  effect on babies of mothers who 112–13
  giving up 68, 86
  going back to 98, 99, 102–4
Wurtzel, Elizabeth 17